Need, Greed or Freedom

John Whitmore was a successful professional racing driver, farmer and businessman before his interest in psychology and science led him to the United States to study and engage in research. In 1980 he returned to England to found a school teaching tennis and skiing by revolutionary new psychological methods. He soon developed similar programmes for performance improvement in business, which are now provided through Performance Consultants, a group of training professionals who specialize in coaching and teambuilding. He is the author of many articles on a wide variety of subjects and three books, the most recent of which is the business bestseller *Coaching for Performance*, now in ten languages.

by the same author

The Winning Mind
Superdriver
Coaching for Performance

Need, Greed or Freedom

Business Changes and Personal Choices

John Whitmore

ELEMENT
Shaftesbury, Dorset • Rockport, Massachusetts
Brisbane, Queensland

© Element Books Limited 1997
text © John Whitmore 1997

First published in Great Britain in 1997 by
Element Books Limited
Shaftesbury, Dorset SP7 8BP

Published in the USA in 1997 by
Element Books Inc.
PO Box 830, Rockport, MA 01966

Published in Australia in 1997 by
Element Books Limited for
Jacaranda Wiley Limited
33 Park Road, Milton, Brisbane 4064

Design by Lansdell Associates
Cover design by Slatter-Anderson
Typeset by Lansdell Associates
Printed and bound in Great Britain by
Biddles Limited, Guildford and King's Lynn

British Library Cataloguing in Publication Data available

Library of Congress Cataloging in Publication Data available

ISBN 1–85230–945–8

Contents

List of Figures

List of Tables

Credits

The author and publishers would like to thank the following for permission to use their cartoons:

    Los Angeles Times syndicate, p 51
    John Maunder, p 55
    The Washington Post, p 99
    Wally Fawkes (Trog) and *The Observer*, p 104

Thanks are also due to Syd Field for permission to use the diagram on p 21.

The extract from *Maverick* by Ricardo Semler, © 1993 by Tableturn, Inc, published by Century, is reproduced by permission of the author c/o Rogers, Coleridge & White Ltd, 20 Powis Mews, London W11 1JN.

Special thanks are also due to the following for permission to use their material extensively:

    Roger Harrison
    Paul Hawken
    Francis Kinsman

Acknowledgements

The subject matter of this book is so broad that the list of people who have contributed to it indirectly is endless. I thank you all, and name just a few. Esther Anderson first challenged me to find myself by asking me who I was, behind the mask of my sporting success and my inherited position and possessions. The question triggered a crisis of identity, a dose of meningitis and a huge appetite for reading. Thereafter Dick Price and others at Esalen Institute continued my psychological awakening. Jim Garrison's insights and the courage of the people of Central America contributed much to my political awakening. Jim Hurtak, Roberto Assagioli and Phyllis Schlemmer did their best to awaken me spiritually. Tim Gallwey of Inner Game fame further opened my eyes to unexplored riches within, and also the door to my current career.

I can trace the origin of this book back to 1978 when Graham Wilson allowed me to write a series of articles entitled 'Models of Change' for his magazine *New Life*, a by-product of the Festival for Mind, Body and Spirit in London. After a breakfast conversation with Bernard Levin a couple of years ago, I first put pen to paper. Francis Kinsman, both personally and through his book *Millennium*, inspired me to keep going. Hazel Henderson greatly encouraged me after reading my first draft. My colleagues at Performance Consultants gave me time, space, support – and some critical feedback.

Brian Dunnigan kept an eye on my political correctness. Nick Lennard, Jane Kent and Paul Stevens helped me to manage my computer. Michael Mann of Element Books was brave enough to take on this book, and me. Sally Lansdell Yeung, my editor, cleaned up my logic and my language. My wife Diana not only encouraged and supported me throughout, but also kept me from going over the top and on the right psychological track. My effervescent 13-year-old son Jason, my independent daughter Tina, living in America, and my feisty

92-year-old mother, who in the midst of great adversity invariably exclaims 'Aren't we lucky', each in their own way reinforce my belief that our own family members can be our greatest teachers, if we allow them to be.

I dedicate this book to Jason and to all those young people who will be coming into their prime at the millennium. I believe they will master need and greed, and find freedom far more successfully than my generation has done. I have no doubt that they will leave the world a better place for their children than we have left it for them.

Introduction

Need, greed and freedom are possibly the three most potent and pervasive forces in our world today. One-third of the 5.5 billion inhabitants of our planet are constantly and gravely in **need** of the basics of life, while the so-called developed world is driven by, and even dependent on, **greed** as a way of life. We speak of the consumer society, market forces, capitalism, but call it what you will, euphemisms cannot conceal the inescapable reality. That there is inequitable distribution and consumption of the world's resources is undeniable. That we do possess sufficient resources, and the means to deploy them, is also unarguable. What we lack is the personal and political will to do so.

Business leaders and big corporations wield real power in the world today but they lack the vision to carry them, and us, beyond their short-term commercial imperatives. This book is a call for all the stakeholders of the business community – meaning all of us – to wake up to the opportunities, the pitfalls and the responsibilities that are facing us. Tough but hugely rewarding choices lie ahead, if we open our eyes and our minds.

A significant change for the good may be on the horizon. What is the nature of this change, and how far is the horizon? The taller we stand, the greater our vision. The farther we look, the closer and clearer that change draws. And there are no losers from this change, so there is nothing to fear but the loss of our chains and our own fear. For both organizations and individuals, change is in the air, and it is more than just hope – it is **freedom** we seek.

Freedom, like **need** and **greed**, is both a physical condition and a state of mind. Our state of mind individually and collectively defines and determines our physical condition, and that of those around us. We live in the prison of our own thinking. We yearn for **freedom**, be it **freedom** from grinding **need**, freedom from the pointless and end-less rat race or freedom from the imperatives imposed on us by our society and by ourselves. True **freedom** is an aspiration for all, but a reality for so few.

These three forces of need, greed and freedom can be understood more readily if we examine the individual and collective thought patterns which underlie them. We can thereby reduce them to something less overpowering and paralysing, to something we can dare to think about, because it is within our power to do something about them. The notion that need, greed and a lack of freedom are just part of the human condition, are just human nature and always will be, is a lie that saves us from having to take responsibility.

Until we find freedom,

   we will have greed.

   So long as we're greedy,

   they will be needy.

How then do we all contribute to **need** and **greed**, and how and where do we find **freedom**? In this brief book it would be outrageously presumptuous of me to provide the answers, but I am going to suggest where we might look for those answers. I will attempt to make some sense of what is going on in our world, our nation, our society, our community, our team at work or at play, and even within ourselves. To make sense of anything demands that we understand or perhaps create an order from what appears to be random, spontaneous or chaotic.

The bad news

In a world in which events are increasingly shaped by selective and sensationalized reporting, deducing the truth from soundbites and tabloid headlines is no easy task and few can be bothered to dig deeper. Is it surprising that we have lost faith in politicians who flounder in reaction to people and events rather than governing them? Is it surprising that not only captains of industry but whole industries are swept along by unpredicted economic tides? Is it so surprising that social, racial, sexual, religious and cultural groupings break down and reform ever more quickly? We have come to expect the worst so much that even small and tentative steps towards peace and reconciliation are hailed as breakthroughs – before they disappoint.

The United Nations could not cope with Saddam Hussein, Somalia, Rwanda, Bosnia or Chechnya; the United States does not have the will to cope with gun crime. Child abuse, rape and unspeakable violence abound in society, on television, in videos and in computer games. Drug-related death is dealt out in various forms and with relative impunity by the Colombian cartels and the tobacco and pharmaceutical industries alike. For those struggling to survive in government and industry, profits and tax revenue continue to take precedence over the state of our health, education or environment. The symptoms of stress and mental distress are all too apparent in society at large and, if we are honest, among our friends and within ourselves.

The good news

The fact that these kinds of events do not seem to respond to any action we take suggests that they are driven by powerful forces of which we are barely aware. Instead of pushing against the inevitable, if we were able to understand and trust the fundamental thrust of human evolution it might be possible to cooperate with it. Wise counsel is perhaps in order, such as 'Don't push the river' and 'Ride the horse in the direction it is going'.

Dreadful things are happening, but there are also countless examples of the emergence of the human spirit, often in response to horrific tragedies. Some of these have a high profile, such as Live Aid and Mother Teresa, but there are also thousands of less visible collective and individual initiatives being taken daily all over the world to help meet the needs of the poor, the starving and the oppressed. There is an ever more powerful environmental lobby spearheaded by organizations such as Greenpeace and backed by many unseen and unsung heroes whom governments and industry ignore at their peril.

At least child abuse, rape, racial and sexual discrimination, torture, animal suffering and the like are now on the public agenda instead of being ignored or denied as they were only a couple of decades ago. Smokers are becoming more and more isolated, the number of drunk drivers is dwindling and cars are slowly becoming 'greener'. The public is less willing to tolerate unethical business conduct – the Milkens and Maxwells are falling from the top deck. The call for change is being heard most strongly in what might seem to be the least likely places. Some of the largest commercial institutions are just beginning to acknowledge the need fundamentally to change their culture, their management style and their ethics, for change they must if they are to survive. Many embark on the process by doing the right thing for the wrong reasons, but that is the way positive change often starts.

On the international front, the Berlin Wall is down, the Cold War is over. Totalitarianism has failed and even China is taking tentative steps towards adopting less oppressive ways, though not yet over Tibet. There are steps towards peace, if not reconciliation in Bosnia, Northern Ireland and the Middle East. It will take time and there will be setbacks, but there are grounds for hope.

A map

I will be exploring a number of these events and processes in a little more depth in this book but, most importantly, I am going to suggest a framework into which they may be slotted to make sense of their apparently random and often paradoxical or contradictory nature. A framework or model is not the truth but is a simplification or representation of the truth which furthers our understanding.

The body of human knowledge grows, but confusion and disaffection seem to grow too. However, countless tomes, ancient and modern, encyclopaedic and academic, political and analytical, prodigious and religious, evolutionary and revolutionary, fill our public and private libraries, yet every day our world becomes apparently more complex and every day we have less time in which to study and understand its complexities.

Most of us are far too caught up with meeting our deadlines and our personal or our family's needs to try to extract true understanding from the many, often conflicting opinions we come across every day. Consequently, we are carried along by the stream of events, not knowing if we are about to be deposited in a backwater or be swept over the weir. Our lives might be more effective if we had a rudimentary map and a few signposts that would enable us to make choices rather than remaining victims of circumstances. The map I am proposing here may help you to find your way, but the map is not the territory – that you must explore for yourself.

The changes I am mapping in this book are occurring according to a very approximate timescale and the map will not have too many topographical features. You can fill in the gaps. You can discover uncharted areas and correct cartographic errors in the light of your own experience. Like all models, the one offered here is imperfect and incomplete; but it is simple to understand – and it suggests that optimism is in order.

I hope to show that, however joyfully or painfully we each experience our role in the greater human predicament, our ultimate destination, both individually and collectively, is one of peace, harmony and freedom. Though I don't expect to see much of these in my lifetime, it makes it worthwhile to strive towards them for the sake of our children's children.

The map may be used to guide us through some of the great social movements in history, or to plan the future development of our company or sports team, or for our own personal development. It could help politicians to develop some vision beyond party politics and to recognize the origins, and the folly, of their primitive point-scoring behaviour in the House of Commons, the House of Representatives or any other house for that matter. It could help those captains of industry who have already recognized the need for fundamental culture change to understand what they want to change to and why. It could help you to make sense of the turbulent times we live in and thereby to alleviate the oft-felt fear of the unknown. You may find comfort in the notion that the fluctuations we experience are not just random but do follow a pattern.

That pattern itself does not change, cannot be changed, but our journey through it, individually and collectively, will at times be fast and at other times be slow. We may appear to stop or even go into reverse for a while, but this does not negate or deny the inexorable underlying thrust – towards evolution.

1
Positive Evolution

The model which is the theme of this book will be examined in the next chapter. First, I need to explain that it depends on one fundamental premise. That is that evolution occurs, not merely in a Darwinian sense, but, as my dictionary defines it, as 'a process of change in a particular direction'. During a memorable meeting at the BBC many years ago, David Attenborough 'corrected' me by claiming that people do not evolve. To me, not only do people evolve, but so do groups, teams, corporations, cultures, nations and humanity itself. One of the most important fathers of progressive psychology, Roberto Assagioli, asserted that evolution was a reasonable bet and that we should try believing in it. I have, and I do, and that is what this book is about.

A second definition in my dictionary describes evolution as 'the process by which, through a series of steps, something attains its distinctive character'. This suggests that evolution may be driven from within towards a fully developed form, or towards the full manifestation of what that something already and really is. I believe this to be true also.

The value of evolution

Both definitions are careful to avoid putting any value on evolution. Is it a good thing to evolve? Is the evolved thing any better than the unevolved thing? What is 'better' in this case? Back to Darwin, does the survival of the fittest breed 'worse' aggressiveness in the long term? Are the animals of today any better than those of yesteryear? Are people any better than they used to be? Indeed, what is better in any case?

Harmony is, to me at any rate, a better state than disharmony. The current state of our society could hardly be described as harmonious. Was it more harmonious in the past, centuries, millennia ago? Will it become more harmonious at some point in the future? Do you believe that greed, violence, exploitation and aggression are just part of being human, and as such will always be with us in about the same measure as today? Or do you believe, as I do, that human beings are caring and compassionate at their core, but that their essential goodness is concealed by layers of fears, defences and survival strategies assembled in our early years and reinforced as time goes by to protect us. And what are we trying to protect ourselves from? From the unevolved part of each other. The process of evolution can be seen as stripping away these layers to get closer to our core, or to who we really are. If you are sceptical about this optimistic assertion, I hope later chapters will provide persuasive evidence in its support.

Optimism or pessimism?

I am an optimist. To me the proverbial glass is half full, not half empty. I believe that things will get better, but that does not mean that Murphy's law – 'if anything can go wrong, it will' – does not apply many times along the way. That is the paradox of the world we live in. The optimist will look at the rough balance between good and evil, progress and regression, a disaster and the selfless response to it, and celebrate the evolutionary thrust towards harmony within those events. The optimist will look for the best in people, the magnificence of our planet, the beauty of the thunder clouds and the learning in the disaster. The optimist will note the destructiveness, the disharmony and the pain only as the inevitable, but ultimately unsuccessful, reaction against positive evolution.

The pessimist, on the other hand, sees only the bad in the present and holds little hope for the future, often yearning for the 'good old days' of the past. The clouds are a threat and the roof will probably leak, the absence of the timely phone call to announce someone's arrival at a distant destination will be interpreted as evidence of a travel accident. Macro and micro matters alike are given the worst case treatment. Let us look at just one mundane example of collective but inaccurate pessimism which we all too easily get sucked into, the state of traffic and roads in and around London, or any of the world's other major cities.

In the old days of the horse and cart, carriage and hansom cab, the noise of horse shoes and steel rims on the cobbled London streets made uninterrupted sleep almost impossible in some areas. Today we rightly campaign against exhaust pollution in our cities, but did you know that the 50,000 horses in London in the year 1900 daily produced 1,000 tons of horse emissions on the streets, which bred billions of flies and was extremely detrimental to Londoners' health. We complain about hold-ups on the M25, London's notorious orbital motorway, but readily forget how much longer it took to circumnavigate London before it was built. We are appalled at the road accident figures in Britain today, but traffic volume has increased by 10 million vehicles in the 25 years since 1969 and the mileage covered has doubled, yet traffic accident fatalities have fallen by half from 7,365 to 3,650 in the same period and are continuing to fall.

Self-fulfilling prophecies

The pessimist always claims to be a realist, but in this book I hope to demonstrate that pessimism itself is unrealistic, and very unwise. Pessimism may turn out to be a very major force inhibiting positive evolution. The German philosopher Goethe went a step further by suggesting that if we treat people as they are, we are liable to have the negative effect of reinforcing their self-limiting self-perception. On the other hand, he said, if we treat people as they could be, we will help them become that. The evidence for self-fulfilling prophecy, sometimes known as the Pygmalion effect, is overwhelming. An experiment on this phenomenon was conducted more than 20 years ago by Dr Millard Blakely of the University of Michigan. It has been repeated in many different forms by others and the results are invariably similar. Here, for illustrative purposes, is a simplified generic example of such an experiment carried out in the field of education.

A group of 60 academically average children were divided randomly into three classes. A small group of teachers were to teach all the classes a similar curriculum of various subjects for several months. The researchers lied to the teachers by telling them that Class A consisted of all the bright kids in the group, Class B was the average class and Class C comprised slow learners and troublemakers. This was not true. After the experiment the children were academically tested again and Class A now showed above-average performance, while Class C now really did have some slow learners and troublemakers. It is not difficult to imagine how the expectations of the teachers caused them to be interesting and enthusiastic with Class A and boring, repetitive and controlling with Class C with corresponding results.

The outcome of this and similar experiments is predictable and hardly unexpected to most people, but it has enormous implications for educators, parents, managers, the police, the judiciary, the government, for healthcare, for sports performance, for national aspirations and for our own thoughts about ourselves. We can choose to create negative mental images about ourselves and others, as the pessimist does, and soon our pessimism will be justified. Or we can view our potential and the potential of others optimistically, and our positive visions help to create the context in which they may be realized.

When I first started working in management training 15 years ago, I was frequently appalled at the derogatory terms so many managers employed to describe their shopfloor workers. Yes, they got what they deserved and what they asked for. They got the type of workforce that they described. They also got to be 'right', something very important to a weak manager. Their description of their workforce was surprisingly accurate, but how had it become that way? The managers' perspective and negative expectations ensured that their poor workforce remained poor and that the managers had others to blame for their own failures. Fortunately management standards have evolved somewhat since then.

Management is evolving, so is government, so is technology, so is sports performance and so are we, both collectively and individually, provided that we do not get in our own way! All these and more are evolving, and in a positive direction, but the time frame is undetermined, taking little account of individual lifespans, and the power of counter-evolutionary forces frequently causes stalls and even reversals along the way.

Time frames

There is a crucial relationship between what is perceived as positive or negative and the time frame over which the perception is made. Events or trends which look very bad in the short term may well come to be seen as superficial or beneficial if the viewing term is extended. For example in sport, the loss of an important match, a championship or a key player, a disaster at the time, may be recognized and even welcomed by the longer-term observer as holding the potential to galvanize or harmonize the team for greater things in the future.

Likewise, a downturn in the economy or a collapse in housing prices may be traumatic for many individuals, but for society as a whole in the long term it may be a stabilizing, rebalancing necessity. Such fluctuations will be judged very differently when they are looked at through the eyes of a home owner, an estate agent, a politician, an economist or a social historian, partly because of their degree of involvement and partly because of their viewing time frame. Of course, some social historians who also have large mortgages may be schizophrenic in their attitudes to this phenomenon.

Just as politicians choose the statistics and the method of illustrating them which presents them to the public in the best or worst light according to their purpose and political colour, they also select their time frames to their best advantage. Whenever a politician tells us how much progress has been made since such and such a year, it is worth looking at the statistics for the previous year, if it was in that party's stewardship. They almost invariably show the opposite trend. Never believe a politician!

The time frame through which we view education, whether it is to meet industry's immediate needs or whether it is for the long-term development of the potential of individuals, will cause our value judgements of it to vary widely. My 13-year-old son is a promising tennis player. The training needs which will help him to succeed at 16 are different from an ideal, longer-term plan for him to peak at, say, 20. Most juniors and their parents take the short-term view, but my son and I have heeded the advice of a wise old coach who counselled us that tennis is a marathon not a match. Both of us now view his current ups and downs, his wins and losses, differently and far more positively. He has gained confidence and consequently his performance and his learning have both improved.

If evolution does occur in a positive direction, the longer-term view will always be more positive. My own optimism stems, in part at least, from the fact that I take a very long-term view, sometimes one which extends far beyond my own lifetime. However, doing this is much harder for self-centred people whose judgement of what is good and bad is based on how things affect them personally and immediately. I hope to show later that people are beginning to evolve beyond that less productive way of being. Education, government and commerce are also showing the early signs of a similar maturing as wider ethical and environmental concerns creep on to their agendas. These have yet to replace profits as a driving force, but all in good time.

2
Inclusion, Assertion and Cooperation

Some readers will be relieved, others disappointed, by the simplicity of the model I am going to present. Any model which is to encompass as much as this one does must be simple, must be a generalization. Its strength lies in the fact that it can embrace such a large part of human experience and yet remain simple enough to be understood, remembered by and useful to the most casual student of life. It can be applied to any organism, group or organization of any size. It can also be built on to form as many complex labyrinths as the most pernickety professor might enjoy. However, this book is for the majority of us who fit somewhere between the two.

The basic developmental model has three stages: *inclusion*, *assertion* and *cooperation*. The words denote the predominant behaviour, need or characteristic of each phase. In the columns beneath these identifying words are other corresponding words or diagrams which indicate associated characteristics *(see* figure 1). They will be explained further in later chapters.

A fourth column is added to allow for various four-stage models. I include the fourth stage of each of these models as a subdivision of the *cooperation* stage. A number of the models make a distinction between the early and later part of the *cooperation* stage because, in the initial phase, individuals and groups can be quite inward looking and precious, even self-satisfied ('Ah, now we have arrived'). Only when that has passed do full potential and *cooperative* effectiveness emerge. For the purposes of this discussion, however, I propose to focus on the three principal stages.

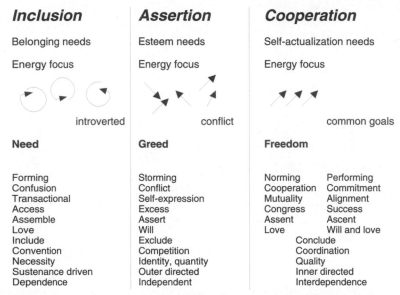

Figure 1: Inclusion, assertion and cooperation compared to other models

Universality

The model suggests that any organism, group or organization passes through each of these stages in its turn on its evolutionary journey. Halts and reversals in the evolutionary progression are commonplace, caused by the changing circumstances and composition of these groupings. We are likely to be far more familiar with the first two of these stages, *inclusion* and *assertion*, for reasons which will become clear. Subsequent chapters will examine how this model applies to the various groups with which people tend to be most involved. Families, work teams, sports teams, common interest clubs, geographical regions, political entities and nations are but a few examples. We shall see that within most groups a number of subgroups form which in turn go through the same developmental sequence but most likely in a different time frame.

Complexity

The development of our personality can be examined in the light of this model, but each of us is comprised of a number of different sub-personalities which are themselves in different stages and moving at different rates. Since our various subpersonalities interact differently with other subpersonalities within other people who are in subgroups of larger groups, and since each of us participates in a considerable number of groups, the potential for complexity becomes very apparent. The inherent simplicity of the model allows us to build it up sequentially to any level of complexity. For the moment, however – and for the sake of our sanity – let's keep it simple.

Inclusion

Anyone who has walked into a room full of strangers and experienced a twinge of discomfort or anxiety knows something about the desire for *inclusion*. The wish to be included, to be accepted, to be one of the group, to blend into the crowd, is accompanied by the fear of rejection. Rejection rarely occurs in these circumstances, but the fear of it is a powerful emotion nevertheless. The bottom line is the very human need to be liked; one way to ensure that we are liked or acceptable is to behave in the same way as others, to conform to group norms. Most of us at some time have experienced the discomfort of being over- or underdressed for a party or a social occasion and found ourselves apologizing for our failure to come in 'uniform'. Our concerns all seem to revolve around our wish to be *included*.

Assertion

When the feared rejection does not occur, and with the passage of time, our *inclusion* concerns subside and another issue rears its head. We begin to want to be someone in the group, to gain the respect or even the admiration of the others. We seek personal recognition and we *assert* ourselves to get it. We may reject or customize the 'uniform' in a desire to express our individuality. We overtly or surreptitiously compete with other group members, try to control the group or even challenge the leadership. What we are consciously or unconsciously competing for is our position in the group hierarchy, the pecking order. In animal terms we are marking out our territory, *asserting* our right to it and perhaps defending it against challengers. We *assert* our independence and we exert our power. These are very different behaviours to the ones we displayed in the *inclusion* stage.

Cooperation

Once we 'know where we stand' in the group, the need to prove ourselves subsides and we become more magnanimous and inclusive. Our concern shifts from self to the group as a whole. Our personal needs may become secondary to the needs of the group. We *cooperate* with and support others rather than compete with them. We will adopt the role that is most needed by the group rather than the one we might otherwise prefer. We trust one another and become more open and honest. Essentially, we choose to *cooperate* with each other for the good of the whole. If this sounds a little idealistic or unrealistic, it is simply that these are far less familiar behaviours to most of us than are the behaviours of the *assertion* stage.

In the following chapters I will flesh out these skeletal characteristics of each of the three phases of group development using examples from various different types and sizes of group. However, you will probably already have observed some of these characteristics in groups with which you have been involved, and you are almost certain to have experienced the desire to be *included* and to *assert* yourself in a group. You may even have wanted to *cooperate* with others on occasion! Take the family as an example.

The family

The most familiar of all groupings is the family, and I am going to use it here to illustrate how we can view group social interaction in terms of the *inclusion– assertion–cooperation* model. It may also help you to interpret some of the reactions you have experienced with your own family. Of course, since I am only using it here for illustrative purposes, I am ignoring the multitude of other behavioural influences that exist in the very complex unit we call the family. It does provide a useful example of our model because the evolutionary cycle keeps repeating itself in a time frame that we can follow. Let us enter the system at the point at which boy meets girl.

Inclusion

Aside from the obvious implications of physical attraction, there is often some desire to couple up on the part of one or both parties. The question in the minds of both young people will be, 'Do I want to be with this person?', 'Could I imagine myself being with him or her more often?', 'Do I like him or her?' and, of course, 'Does he/she like me?'. These are the *inclusion* questions. What about the behaviour?

If they are attracted to one another both parties will be careful in the beginning to conform to what they perceive as the other's norms. Some of that will of course be based on the cultural archetypes or romantic images and ideals associated with couplehood. Their dress, manners, conversation and behaviour will reflect what they think is expected of them by the other. That may include adopting the uniform of the skinhead or the Hell's Angel, country casual or city fashion. In this way each seeks acceptance by and the approval of the other party, even if this means suppressing their own individuality. This is *inclusion* stage behaviour.

Assertion

Once both parties begin to feel safe with one another and once some continuity has been established, each will begin to reintroduce their own habits and preferences, little by little. They will be more cautious in revealing these, especially the odd ones, if their desire for the relationship to succeed is high. We are now into the *assertion* stage. The bumps and clashes begin to occur as each *asserts* how they want to be, how they want the other to be and how they want things to be in their relationship. A few couples will already be married by this point and accusations like 'You were never like this until we got married' are thrown around. This should hardly be surprising, because marriage signifies the end of the courtship or *inclusion* stage.

A few relationships never get beyond the *inclusion* stage. These are generally those which are very unbalanced, often with one party exercising considerable power over the other. The not-so-covert game is, 'You will have to be continually the way I want you to be, or I will reject you' or 'Your desire to be *included* gives me power over you and I am going to use that to my advantage'. Most couples, if they remain together at all, reach the *assertion* stage, and there they remain till death parts the contestants!

Assertion takes a myriad of forms in a relationship: some unconscious, some subtle, some calculated and some violent. I would not attempt to explain all the different marital feuds that occur in terms of a simple three-stage model. However, understanding the existence and the power of *assertion* may help a few couples understand why they fight so fiercely about which end of the toothpaste tube should be squeezed. If they finally recognize that it has nothing to do with toothpaste and everything to do with *assertion*, this book will have been worth the effort.

The need to *assert* ourselves, and the fact that this appears with our theoretical nearest and dearest, is perhaps a measure of how powerless so many of us feel in the world we have constructed. The vast influences of business, of politics, of economics, of the media and of crime are very effective at demonstrating to us how ineffective each of us is. Where then can we express power with any hope of effect? Sadly, and sometimes tragically, our home and our partner are our only remaining arena. This greatly adds to the force of simple family *assertion* issues.

Back to inclusion
Think for a moment about a couple who have been together for a few years and who are firmly in the *assertion* phase. Along comes a baby. Suddenly we have a new system, *inclusion* issues are back on the menu – and the little angel does not even know that she is an issue. At the very same time as the couple are trying to get used to the fact that there is a new player on the team, the father may begin to feel that it is he who is being excluded. To hell with his old *assertion*

games, now he is concerned whether he still has a place on the team.

And assertion

Typically the mother and child bond and the besotted dad conforms to the archetype and is loving and supportive, in part in order to be *included*. After a while, however, he may begin to *assert* his views of how the child should be brought up and may even *assert* himself against the power he now perceives the baby to possess. Of course, the baby actually has very little of this, but perceived power is very powerful in itself.

This is a little setback in the evolutionary journey of this family, but hopefully a welcome one. *Inclusion* needs are met once more, the baby's needs have been well represented by the mother – and back we go into the *assertion* game. Before the couple have got back to where they were before the happy event, the 'terrible twos' begin. Baby is reaching the *assertion* stage of her first cycle through the three stages of personal development. And *assert* she does with a vengeance! We are now faced with the interplay between the family system's developmental phase and that of the little individual. What we must not forget is that mum and dad are each also at a certain point in their individual evolutionary progression, so the journey is unlikely to be totally smooth.

Cooperation

Our three-stage model couple have now been together for some 20 years and they have survived junior's pubescent eruptions. They have grown tired of fighting about some things and found accommodation on others. They now use aerosol toothpaste and their non-verbal sexual signalling system has resulted in regularity if not spontaneity. He makes her morning coffee and she makes him breakfast. They share more and row less. Genuine support is given in situations that would previously been taken as an opportunity for *assertion*. They are experiencing the first stirrings of the *cooperation* stage.

Crossroads

Their beloved offspring goes off to university and a new cycle begins. The family team has changed again and back we go to *inclusion*. The problems may be exacerbated by the fact that dad is forced to take early retirement. Our new family team is at a crossroads. Is *inclusion* to be the issue, perhaps even a change of partner? Or were they far enough into the *cooperation* stage to carry them through their new circumstances into a joyful retirement, with new-found interest in each other and expanding interests outside the family?

They become more socially involved, not just with their local community but with wider global concerns. They volunteer to help in a risky trouble spot abroad and their life takes on new depth and meaning. Now they have truly entered the *cooperation* stage as their family team is *cooperating* with and supporting the needs of biggest team we know, humanity. They are the lucky ones. The majority of us never make it on to the global team.

Understanding

Most of us will recognize some of the milestones in the progress of this not untypical family. What could they do to smooth over the bumps? First and foremost, a rudimentary understanding of the three stages and their characteristics makes dealing with the issues much more straightforward, since they arise somewhat predictably. It would also help family members to understand that there is nothing unusual or wrong about having *inclusion* concerns or *assertion* claims. Handling them appropriately when they arise is all that matters. There are, of course, specific actions that the family or a counsellor can take to help meet the needs of members for *inclusion* or *assertion*, or to begin to build the qualities associated with the *cooperation* stage.

Story telling

The story of this family is a familiar one, not only in terms of its content but also its structure. Every story has its beginning, its middle and its end – the classic model of narrative as taught to aspiring playwrights everywhere. Every living thing has the same three-act play. Figure 2 shows a chart from *The Screen Writers' Workbook* by Syd Field, which has a striking simplicity and similarity to our three-stage model.

The story:

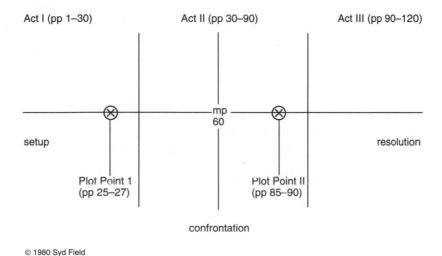

© 1980 Syd Field

Figure 2: The paradigm structured

The words Field uses, set up, confrontation and resolution, could be inserted in the chart at the beginning of this chapter. But note also the two plot points which occur close to the conclusion of the first two acts. The plot points in a play are 'where new information turns the story around in a different pattern'. Likewise, these are the crisis points in our three-stage model when the new impulses begin to come into conflict with and be resisted by the old.

Brian Dunnigan is a senior lecturer in creative writing at the Northern School of Film and Television in Leeds. He comments: 'Three is an archetypal number. It reflects our experience of life – Birth/Growth/Death. And relationship – Overture/Resistance/Consummation. The natural world seems to move in threes. Sunrise/Noon/Sunset. The three phases of the moon – New/Full/Old. Christianity has absorbed these natural facts. Father/Son/Holy Ghost. Creation/Fall/Redemption. It is psychologically satisfying and cathartic.' All these trios can be equated in some way to our three stages. This is perhaps the story of the universe.

Overlapping stages

The family is by no means the only play we have been involved in. Most of us will be able to identify an association with several groups at the same time, and may recognize that we are playing the *assertion* game in one group while being concerned about our mere *inclusion* in another. The personal behaviour characteristics we display with the two groups are really quite different. It is as if we adopt an entirely different subpersonality for each different situation.

The three-stage model proposes that as individual human beings or groups of human beings of any number mature psychologically, a process only very loosely associated with time, they move in turn through each stage and on to the next. Each stage has its attractions which may inhibit people from moving on, and death, inertia, break-downs and regression often intervene before the final stage is reached.

Throughout this book I will superimpose this model on segments of our lives and examine them in the light of three sequential stages. In reality it is not that simple, but maps and models are simple by their very nature and purpose. In fact the borders between the stages are ill defined and social pressures may cause them to shift. None of the stages is wrong, just as a sapling is not wrong for not being a tree; but few would argue against the magnificence of a mature tree. *Cooperation* is a more mature and, in my opinion, more magnificent state than *inclusion* or *assertion*.

Forward movement

However, we need to experience *inclusion* fully, we need to express ourselves through *assertion* during our evolutionary journey. *Cooperation*, if it is to be a true synthesis, does not reject *inclusion* or *assertion* but embraces the good qualities of both. But we can easily become stuck, wallow and indulge ourselves in the less attractive elements of *inclusion* and *assertion*, and thereby inhibit our individual and collective attainment of *cooperation*. I will be particularly hard on *assertion*, not because it is inherently wrong, but because right now there is an excess of it in society, at terrible human cost.

Later we will examine the three-stage model as applied to business teams, but as most of us will at some time or other have played in, or supported, a variety of sports teams, we will look at these next in a little more depth.

3
Sport

The fact that sport has such a high profile today may have something to do with the fact that the dominant global culture, hierarchical materialistic capitalism, is highly competitive by nature. For competitive read *assertive*. So is sport, or at least sport as we know it. Wasn't sport rather more high minded when it was 'invented' by the Greeks? At least we are led to believe it was by the mythology. But the Romans managed to lower the standards by using it as a means of *asserting* their domination over their victims. The Soviet Union saw sport as an arena in which to *assert* its position as a world power, and dominate it did, by fair means and foul. Wasn't the space race a form of sport – with military overtones? So sport offers countless opportunities for self-expression, self-esteem, *assertion* and aggression.

Heroes

Our sports stars are rewarded, watched and worshipped by millions. The pressure to perform is very high – and failure is very visible. There is not much room at the top and not much time there for those who stumble. The sacrifices and commitment demanded to reach the pinnacle are huge. Self-motivation is implicit and essential, yet sport offers huge external rewards or motivators in terms of glamour, fame or money which may divert or distort the focus of attention. The highs are higher, the falls are harder and the lows are lower than they are in many other of life's endeavours. Sport, at least at a professional level, is like life in a pressure cooker.

We dream of emulating our sports heroes. Countless children, often driven by pushy parents, strive to follow in their footsteps with little idea of the investment required economically and emotionally, or of the odds against their success. Perhaps that is a good thing, because if they did know they might never start, and there is still much to be gained by the many who go for it all the way in their hearts, but only some of the way on the road. Most never make it to the top by the black or white rules of the tabloids, but thousands succeed according to more subtle criteria.

Fans

And then there are the watchers, the enthusiasts, the fans and the collectors of all manner of sports paraphernalia, from replica Jaguar D-types to Andre Agassi T-shirts. Whole industries thrive on producing look-alike clothing. Half the population wears shell suits beyond their years, their purses or their girths, and we all wear trainers, though most of us would run a mile to avoid using them for their designated purpose. Of course, vicarious or armchair sport does not go far enough to satisfy the *assertion* need, but for many it may well meet their *inclusion* or belonging needs.

Participating

Assertion needs are met by *asserting* ourselves – and by doing so successfully – or by psychotherapy! But wait: there is hope for us all. Taking part, playing the game, running the race, doing one's best, going for it – this is success, this is the name of the game for many people. Nowhere is this better illustrated than in the participation by those of all abilities, shapes and ages in marathons all over the globe. Participation meets *inclusion* needs for everyone and, for those who do really go for it, whatever their result, their *assertion* needs are met as well. In the major marathons there are very few losers – only those who see themselves as losers do in fact lose. However, going for it with all you have brings its own incomparable private reward.

Sport provides a great deal of fulfilment to the many who play, who strive to achieve their best, who win club, county, regional or national competitions, but who will never stand on an Olympic rostrum. Self-esteem and some large egos are built on the tracks and playing fields by the winners, but if that is the only game there will inevitably be more losers than winners. The best coaches and sport organizers are forever trying to devise ways of increasing the proportion of winners with leagues, handicaps, modified scoring systems, forfeits and the like. Competitions often have first-round losers' play-offs, narrow age bands, runner-up prizes and rewards for effort, improvement, achievement and excellence which are unquantifiable and therefore subjectively selected, but they are all ways of giving more people something to go for and something to gain.

The Inner Game

'Winning is everything,' says Linford Christie, and he is right if *assertion* over others is everything; but it isn't. 'Winning isn't everything, but losing isn't anything,' as Schultz pointed out in the comic strip *Peanuts*. It all depends on whether we are referring to the outer game, the inner game or even a combination of the two. The inner game was most clearly defined by Tim Gallwey, author of *The Inner Game of Tennis* and several other books, when he suggested that in tennis 'the opponent in one's own head is more formidable than the one on the other side of the net'. Only one person wins the point, but all competitors have the opportunity to win the inner game every time they play, by mastering their own internal obstacles. Full self-expression is the name of the inner game.

Motivation

Sport offers so many people a forum for self-expression, which is the most refined form of *assertion* and is entirely positive and healthy. What does self-expression really mean? It is the outward manifestation of our full potential. This would seem to be closer to the qualities of the *co-operation* stage than those of *assertion*. It has to be remembered that the three stages are not separated by hard or impermeable boundaries.

Self-expression bridges the *assertion* and *cooperation* stages in the following way. Periods of *assertion* are normal and necessary in an individual's development, but they can also be seen as self-serving and divisive. Early in the *assertion* stage people will see themselves as different from, in comparison to, in competition with or opposed to others. As their fuller potential begins to emerge, self-expression is experienced as inseparable from and in *cooperation* with the greater whole. This shift parallels the evolution from acquiring esteem from others, to building self-esteem, a concept which is elaborated in the next chapter.

Competition versus *cooperation*

The stronger and uglier the manifestations of *assertion* are in our society and in sport, the more vociferous the anti-competition lobby becomes. It has an important policing role to play, but it is populated by people who have felt or seen the losing end of competition in school or elsewhere and who do not value the counter-balancing benefits or the essential evolutionary nature of *assertion*.

For the young and the young at heart, sport is an ideal, and relatively safe, way of meeting their *assertion* needs. If this need can be achieved through simulation in sport, then there is often less need for *assertiveness* to be expressed destructively at work, at home or in teams later. Of course, people who have very large *assertion* needs, however outstandingly they perform in sport, will probably have plenty left over to express in life. An observer might comment that such people are taking the aggression they learn on the sports field into life, therefore sport is bad; but who knows how aggressive that person might have been had their sport not been an outlet for a considerable portion of that energy?

Those who are not fortunate enough to have the opportunity or encouragement to participate in sport may find partially or wholly anti-social ways of expressing their *assertion* needs. It is not surprising that these often occur around the periphery of sport. Soccer hooliganism is perhaps the most obvious and aggressive example, but the temptation and the tendency for young bloods to leave a motor racing

Grand Prix in their noisy sports cars like hooligans is only curbed by
the sheer volume of traffic. I know – I was one of them in my youth!

Responsibility

Sports stars carry a heavy responsibility as they can not avoid becoming role models. Unfortunately, and occasionally fortunately, fans do
not always emulate the behaviour of their hero but what they perceive, often erroneously, to be his or her winning attributes. They are
more likely to perceive aggression, or unrefined *assertion*, rather than
self-expression or comradeship. There is no single or easy answer to
such questions as:

❑ Does professional sport provide a good example for children?
❑ Do sport and competition encourage aggression or act as a safety valve for
   its harmless release?
❑ Does sport make us care more or less about others in the game?
❑ Does sport harden us to physical violence or make us more aware and caring of physical vulnerability?
❑ If most sports are beneficial in these terms, can we also give the benefit of
   the doubt to WWF wrestling, boxing, paintball war games? And what about
   violent video games?
❑ Where is the line, or is it possible to draw one at all, between what is healthy
   and what is not?

I suspect, like most things, that the answers depend on the individual,
on where he or she is in terms of personal development and on that
elusive thing called balance.

The sports team

It was necessary to start by exploring a little about how individuals
relate to sport, but in this book we are primarily concerned with collective or team behaviour. Sports teams characterize the behaviour of

the many less obvious teams in which we participate, which is why sport can be such a great training ground for learning how to work together. Teamwork in sport is expected to reach the highest quality in the minimum of time, and often the most successful are those who work best as a team, rather than those who possess outstanding skill. An example of this was the Great Britain field hockey team who won the gold medal in the Seoul Olympics in 1988. The same might have been said about the England rugby team in the early 1980s, at the time of Bill Beaumont and Roger Utley.

The challenge for sports team managers and coaches is high, yet few of them have any training in group process beyond common sense and their own previous experience as competitors. That does not mean that they can not find success. They do, but it is somewhat hit and miss. Relative success is often achieved, but the majority of sports teams fall far short of their potential. We accept this shortfall only because most of us have rarely if ever experienced anything better. Seldom have I seen any sports team operate consistently in the *cooperation* stage of team development; most never make it all the way through *assertion*.

Let's look at some examples from sport of each of the three phases of team development, and in particular consider what the manager or coach can do to foster team cohesion and performance.

We can start from the premise that a team well established in the *cooperation* stage would perform better than the same team in either of the two earlier stages. It follows, therefore, that a primary function of a sports manager or coach is to speed the team's progress to that stage. They have other functions as well, such as skill development, fitness training, strategy and team tactics, and organizational and probably financial management. These all place great demands on the coach's time and energy, but can be so much easier to handle if the team is truly *cooperative*.

Group process

It is for this reason that I would start, given a free hand and a new team, with group process at quite a deep and intensive level. A number of exercises more frequently used in group therapy would accelerate team development through the stages (*see* chapter 12), but some more reserved team members might not wish to participate. Forcing them to do so, leaving them out or making them out to be wrong for not doing so would be divisive and totally counter-productive, so it would be better to drop the idea if their reservations can not be assuaged. They may well be afraid of their own emotions, disclosure and embarrassment, but they are unlikely to acknowledge this and may not even be conscious of it. Instead they will trot out other arguments such as: 'What is the point?', 'This has nothing to do with football', 'Better to spend our time doing something useful', and 'Oh, I'm not afraid of that touchy feely stuff, I just think it's silly'.

If all team members are willing, however, a day at the outset spent off the sports field on group process can go a long way towards dissolving the *inclusion* fears and confront and meet many of the *assertion* needs in a healthy, open and honest way. Qualities of the *cooperation* phase, such as trust, mutual support, appreciation of differences, openness and honesty, can begin to be established.

Inclusion

Inclusion concerns are likely to be raised in sports teams during the process of squad and team selection. Late selection provides no time for the necessary adjustment to the new team composition and performance can easily suffer as a result. A case in point was in the 1992 Barcelona Olympics in the 4 × 100 metre relay, when the British team composition and running order were only finalized shortly before the event. In spite of the team theoretically being very strong (Adam, Jarrett, Regis and Christie), it was one of the rare occasions on which Britain did not win an Olympic 4 × 100 relay medal; at least prior to the disappointing showing in the Atlanta Olympics in 1996.

The star system

The star system and hierarchy in many soccer teams are aspects of the *assertion* game, but they also have the effect of maintaining uncertainty and compliance among the players who are not confident of their *inclusion*. One soccer manager always had a couple of teenagers 'on trial' on his team. 'This is your one big chance to get into the big time,' he would warn them. At the same time he told his more senior players, 'Watch out, if you are not on your toes these youngsters will take your place.' The consequent widespread fear of being dropped killed creativity and risk taking, and put everyone on their best behaviour, something which made the manager's job easier but it did nothing for team performance.

Attractive as it is to have one or more star players on the team, there are risks. At best they will perform well and inspire others to raise their game; but at worst, especially if they display any arrogance, they can have the effect of demoralizing their fellow team members and causing the break-up of the team. If there is a star player on the team it pays to have also at least a couple of really solid team players with plenty of fire but no fireworks for the other team members to identify with.

No sports team, or any other team, is likely to be perfect. The best managers do their selection early, thoughtfully and intuitively, and then stick with their choices, for better or for worse or until change becomes the only way forward. Only in this way will the players develop trust in their manager and the willingness fearlessly to give their all.

Assertion

Assertion manifests itself in team sports in many ways, such as holding on to the ball, the failure to pass until too late or the attempt at heroic solo scoring. There is no doubt that some team members are more concerned about their own apparent success than about that of the team. They would prefer to be the hero of a match they lost, rather than a solid, supportive player in the match the team won. It is well known that the man to beat in Grand Prix motor racing is your own team mate. He is, after all, in an identical car, unlike the other drivers in the race, and so the race is head to head with no mechanical excuses.

Posturing against other team members can even turn to physical violence, the crudest form of *assertive* behaviour, but there are many more subtle ways in which team members unsettle or undermine their erstwhile team mates, so they can rise above them in the hierarchy, in the estimation of the fans or on the pay scale. Overly zealous negotiation for more favourable contract clauses than those of other team members are as often motivated by the need to *assert* as by a genuine need for the clause. Players with strong *assertion* needs may challenge the coach or team captain in a power struggle. The waste of energy and loss of focus caused by this sort of activity are severely detrimental to team effectiveness, and are very common.

Cooperation

Many of the management and coaching practices employed in the traditional team sports such as soccer, rugby, cricket and hockey unwittingly delay the evolutionary thrust through the *inclusion* and *assertion* phases. One coach who broke from the mould and developed his team to deliver exceptional results was David Whitaker, the coach to the victorious Great Britain field hockey team. Here in his own words is some of the backgound to his Olympic success.

> As often happens in life, an opportunity enables you to develop your own ideas on how something can best be done, even though those ideas are not fully formed at the outset. This is what happened to me with regard to team building during the late 1970s and early 1980s.
>
> I had been involved as a team member in high-performing teams and I had been intrigued at my own feelings and needs as those teams grew in both cohesion and achievement. It was also interesting to note what was happening – and not happening – in the teams which did not quite perform to expectation or potential.
>
> As a result of my personal experiences and observations of others, I took the role of coach to the Great Britain men's hockey team in the 1984–8 Olympic cycle with a much clearer picture not only of the needs of players and team as they were to develop through the natural steps towards being a high-performing team, but also of the ways in which I

could positively facilitate the process.

This cooperation phase was characterized by behaviours which related to 'what we did as hockey players' (eg adaptability, personal skills) and 'how we worked together' (eg mutual respect, honesty, personal responsibility). Our ambition was to achieve the core performance factors to as high a standard as possible (ie 8–10 on a 10-point scale).

However, few of the team members were starting in the cooperation phase and we had to face the reality that most would be involved in inclusion and assertion issues.

Players would be considering questions such as:

❏ Will I be good enough?
❏ What is expected of me?
❏ Will I be accepted by the more senior players?
❏ Will I give a good account of myself?
❏ Who are my main competitors for a position on the team?
❏ How can I get a more central role than before?
❏ How do I establish myself as a valued player in this squad?

The challenge we faced was to help our players answer these questions while at the same time providing a team focus so that the energy and behaviours were moving both individuals and the team towards the cooperation phase.

There are many things a manager can do to foster the speedy evolution of the team through the *inclusion* and *assertion* stages of its development into *cooperation*, and to maintain it when it gets there. There are also many things a team manager can do, with good intent but with disastrous results, that will prevent a team from developing as it could and should. On the next page are some of David Whitaker's observations and recommendations.

❑ Individuals have to choose to be cooperative, so keep a clear focus on individual needs.

❑ Promote ownership, because they must believe in what they are doing.

❑ Continually involve the players in their own learning and develop new ideas with them.

❑ Be receptive to their ideas.

❑ Encourage players to share their views in meetings.

❑ Act as a facilitator in group work, both in meetings and in training.

❑ Give time to individual players as equally as possible.

❑ Recognize that competition, conflict and subgroups are natural processes in team development and focus on promoting the positive outcomes (rather than the well-known negative outcomes) from these situations.

❑ Retain the vision of us being the best team in the world.

❑ Look for learning/growth from every situation, however painful!

❑ High-performing teams cannot be assembled like a car, they need to evolve.

❑ The team needs to be able to perform on the pitch with minimum interference from the coach.

Teams do not come to the cooperation phase in a smooth production-line process, nor do they stay there once achieved! There are, and probably need to be, peaks and troughs in their growth. The aim is to keep the progress onward and upward in both performance and interpersonal processes.

Complex teams

I am also fortunate enough to have spent part of my life as a professional sportsman. I was a racing driver in the 1960s, driving for a variety of private and factory teams. Teamwork was much more haphazard in those days, but I drove for one team leader who was notably better than the rest. He managed to get his team of

individualistic and assertive drivers to *cooperate* remarkably well most
of the time. How he cared for and managed the mechanics was directly
reflected in how they cared for my car and put up with my competition
neuroses. In a single year, 1965, the three teams that he ran, and that I
drove for, won one World Manufacturers' Championship, one
European Drivers' Championship, both in long-distance racing, and
came within a few seconds of winning the Monte Carlo Rally as well.
Thirty years later I recall every member of the team with great affection.

The complexity, the skills, the risks, the schedules, the astronomi-
cal costs and the egos that have to be managed in a motor racing team
are about as extreme as they can get, and yet anyone who has
watched a 7-second tyre and fuel stop in a motor racing Grand Prix
cannot help but be awestruck by the efficiency of the teamwork. The
mechanics are truly the unsung heroes of motor racing who perform
prodigious feats of fast engine changes and overnight rebuilds that
make your local dealership look like a clutch of dead snails!

They seldom see their families, get a good night's sleep, receive any
public acknowledgement or even get to experience the far-away
places to which they travel. They get paid, most of them quite well,
but that is not what makes them do a good job. They do it well
because to them there is no other way to do a job. Nevertheless, it
takes a good manager to keep a team operating at that level, especially one composed of the individualistic types who would do such
a crazy job.

In the 1960s team drivers tended to be very supportive of one
another both in and out of the car, something that is not the case in
Grand Prix racing today. Perhaps it was because the very high attri-
tion rate of drivers at the time provided us with a common external
threat which helped bind us together. With the advent of comprehensive new safety technology and regulations for cars and circuits in
the 1970s and 1980s that common bond was lost, and with it much
of the camaraderie between drivers of the same team and even of
opposing teams. This is neither universally true, nor is it a cry for
deregulation, nor is safety the only reason for the change, but it is
undoubtedly a factor in the decline in supportiveness; and money is
surely another.

Money

I am all for pay in sport, because to perform well one has to train and prepare on a full-time basis, homes and families have to be preserved and preparation for subsequent long-term careers may have to be suspended. Again, it is not the pay that makes a true performer. Most would do it if they were paid or not and many would even pay to do it, because they love to compete in their chosen game, win or lose. Unfortunately, because of the agenda of commercial sponsorship in so many sports, the differential in rewards between, say, the number one and the number five is far too high, and that certainly has a divisive effect. A concentration on money just makes it harder for managers to keep team members focused on the less material, more mental motivational factors that really create outstanding teams who give outstanding performances. What it comes down to is: 'If I offer you a carrot to do a job, what is your attention focused on, the job or the carrot?'

Sport is a microcosm of the world, and one in which participants can learn a great deal about life and about themselves. It is very much about teamwork, but in every sport there is also a very strong individual component. The next chapter examines another model which parallels our three-stage model, but which applies particularly to individuals and which may help explain the hunger to win.

4
Maslow's Model

One of the fathers of the more progressive humanistic psychology being practised today was Dr Abraham Maslow, head of psychology at Brandeis University and a president of the American Psychological Association. In his attempt to understand more about the nature of human beings, he broke with the tradition of studying pathology and instead studied people whom he considered to be psychologically healthy, mature and fulfilled. In his book *Management and Motivation*, published in 1952, he postulated the existence of what he called a hierarchy of needs to which the vast majority of human beings conform. He claimed that we are driven to meet the first category of human needs, and only when those are met will we switch our attention to the next need up the hierarchy, and so on. His hierarchy is closely related to our three-stage model, as figure 3 shows.

The hierarchy of human needs

One can roughly equate Maslow's top three needs of belonging, esteem and self-actualization with the three stages of *inclusion, assertion* and *cooperation*. However, Maslow differentiated between the need for 'esteem from others' and the more elevated 'self-esteem'. Self-esteem and its sibling self-expression can also be as *cooperative* as they are *assertive* in nature. We could say that they lie on the cusp between *assertion* and *cooperation*. It is also easy to see that belonging, safety and shelter, and food, water and sex all fit into the category of need. They are the most basic needs for physical and psychological subsistence.

It is equally possible to argue that the esteem and self-actualization

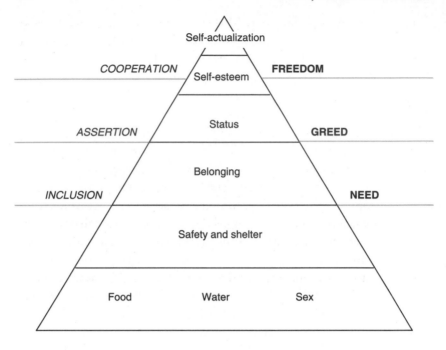

Figure 3: Maslow's hierarchy of needs

needs are not needs at all but a bonus, if not a luxury. Maslow implied, however, that they are needs because only a self-actualized person is complete and mature; and since this was in fact unachievable, he always used the term self-actualiz*ing*. The need of a self-actualizing person is for meaning and purpose; more about which later. Maslow postulated that all the levels of need are developmental stages through which we each inevitably have to pass before becoming complete and mature. The less fortunate might say that the opportunity to pass through them would be a fine thing.

This model has been widely accepted as valid and has been used extensively in many fields that draw on psychology, such as education, management training and relief work in developing countries. To some it may be old hat; others may question the universality of its application. Of course, it must be remembered that models are not absolute but merely serve as guidelines to help us order our thinking. Maslow's model has survived with flying colours.

The hierarchy was challenged by Dr Viktor Frankl, a psychiatrist who spent a considerable time in a Nazi prison camp during the Second World War. He pointed out that, though none of their basic survival needs were met, those who gave away even what little they had tended to survive better than those who stole extra. They had found meaning in helping others, and that in turn gave them the strength or the purpose for survival. The implication here is that, though the hierarchy of needs illustrates the most common behaviour, it is possible to transcend need and leapfrog into self-actualization. The same transcendence occurs when a group faces a crisis. Personal needs are set aside and the now *cooperative* group rises to the occasion. The sad thing is that in most cases, when the crisis subsides so does the *cooperation*. Auschwitz was certainly a crisis and a prolonged one at that.

We will now examine each of these levels of need in more depth.

Physiological needs

Our body automatically attempts to maintain homeostasis (balance) in terms of nutrients, fluids, temperature etc, and we have sensing mechanisms – hunger, thirst, sensitivity to hot and cold etc – to encourage us to satisfy the demands of homeostasis. However, not all physiological needs are homeostatic ones. There are, for example, sexual and sensual needs and needs for sleep and exercise, as well as the converse tendency towards laziness and inertia.

Physiological needs clearly take precedence over all other needs and thus form the base of our hierarchical triangle. Even if none of their other needs are satisfied, starving people are likely to see happiness as having enough to eat. Food and how to acquire it will dominate their thoughts and actions. They will even sacrifice other needs such as freedom to obtain food. Maslow wrote, 'It is quite true that man lives by bread alone – when there is no bread. But what happens to man's desires when there is plenty of bread and his belly is chronically filled?' The answer is that he moves on to the next-level needs, which are loosely categorized as safety needs.

Safety and shelter needs

In the western world, we have little real experience of being deprived of our physiological needs, nor of our more obvious physical needs such as clothing and shelter. The welfare state, a little permissiveness, parents, pensions and the police conspire between them to meet these basic needs for the vast majority. Of course some fall through the net, and if we suddenly lose our job we may momentarily fear for our survival – 'How are we going to feed and clothe the kids and pay the mortgage?' – but not so many of us actually end up on the streets.

Safety needs, however, go beyond the immediate physical necessities. If people's safety is in doubt, they may see everything in terms of safe and unsafe. Because we are taught to inhibit our reactions to threat, the fear of perceived danger is less apparent in adults than in children, who respond instantly to sudden stimulation such as thunder; but these reactions exist nonetheless. However, it is also true that the more stable and secure the upbringing of a child has been, the less disturbance will be caused to that child by an unusual sudden stimulation. Likewise, secure adults will have less need to surround themselves with long-term work contracts, pension schemes and insurance policies, or to choose a political party with a strong commitment to 'national defence'. It can be seen from this that needs can be real or imagined.

Belonging needs

We all have belonging needs, and they are not fully met by even the most embracing of families. How do we meet them outside the family? Even before adolescence we seek to identify with peers and heroes. We support a particular football team and 'they' become 'we', even though the team may never have heard of us. We become attached to a rock star, a film star or a sports star. We may even seek out a fan club to join with others of like mind. We want to be in fashion, not because of a predilection for a particular type of clothing, but in order to be acceptable to our peer group. We join special interest groups or clubs collecting everything from butterflies to Bugattis and all kinds of shared memorabilia.

Few group members would ever recognize or acknowledge it, but the grouping impulse may come far more from the subconscious need to belong than from interest in the subject around which the club was formed. Many of these clubs demand that new members are proposed, seconded and elected, but the club secretary is usually happy to fix that provided that you send in your first subscription. Nevertheless, it remains an important part of the belonging ritual that we are actually chosen!

Orphans or children from broken homes are likely to have more unmet belonging needs than the more fortunate of us, and they may react to this by joining many groups, even those in which they really have little interest, or by defensive denial of this need and becoming highly independent. Our work may form the focus of our communal or belonging life, as in fishing or mining communities whose way of life we defend vigorously. We may become fiercely nationalistic about our locality, our county or our country. Political leaders often try to appeal to our belonging needs, for example by trying to keep 'us' in Britain separate from 'them' in Europe.

Urbanization, the ease and speed of travel, the loss of village social life in the last few decades and the global refugee problem have posed some threat to the satisfaction of belonging needs in society. Perhaps in response to these changes, some sad and all too often ugly manifestations of belonging have emerged, such as extreme nationalism, fundamentalism, soccer violence, and the rave and drug culture.

Esteem needs

Maslow differentiated between the need for esteem from others and that for self-esteem. More than is the case with the other needs these two overlap, and what is seen is a gradual shift from a person's need for prestige, status, attention and adulation from others towards achievement, adequacy, confidence and independence. To avoid confusion, I will use the word status to mean esteem from others in the remainder of this book.

Status

Once people have discovered which groups they belong to and found
acceptance and friends, they may begin to compete with others in the
group. Who has the best collection? Who can win the *concours d'élé-
gance* or the club tournament? Perhaps they seek leadership roles, try
to get elected on to the committee or offer to organize the club fête.
Status is the engine of material acquisition and display. People spend
a fortune acquiring things that they think will give them status, prestige and recognition.

Psychological blocks to progression up the hierarchy cause people
to maximize rather than optimize the physical symbols of security or
success. It is apparent that those who lack self-esteem, often for good
reasons, are the ones who strive hardest for recognition from others.
Ironically, people who have a need to display their opulence may, by
doing so, actually be exhibiting their inadequacy rather than gaining
the prestige they seek. For example, it is the psychologically deprived
part of a person, not the healthy part, which encourages him or her
to pay £180,000 for a Rolls-Royce Corniche or an Aston Martin
Vantage for the sake of status! The trouble is, even that does not work
because esteem is a psychological need which cannot be met vicariously outside one's head. So £180 spent with a psychotherapist might
do their esteem needs more good…

The quest for fame and fortune may drive people to cheat, steal
and even kill to gain recognition. Notoriety in prison is better than
being no one. Athletes who use steroids and other performance-
enhancing substances do not care how they win their recognition, but
it is shallow and short lived because it leads to self-deprecation as
opposed to self-esteem.

Self-esteem

Self-esteem can neither be bought nor stolen. It is not surprising that
so many superstars of stage, screen and rock fame, especially those
with more fans than talent, are prone to suicide attempts. The hol-
lowness of their fame is so painfully apparent to them. Better dead
than famous for what they are not.

Many sports performers are driven by their esteem needs, which
serve as a powerful motivator, more powerful than money in many

cases. To the majority of professional sports people, money soon becomes more significant as a measure of achievement than as a means of life support and acquisition. The adulation of the fans, so intoxicating in the early days, may later become more of an intrusion, or at minimum the necessary price of achievement. The performer looks less for status, the esteem of others, and more for self-esteem. The standards of self-esteem are higher; there is no one to deceive but oneself, and no one to cheat. Only perfection will do. Perfectionists are invariably driven by the need for self-esteem.

Underlying achievement is so often the unrequited need for self-esteem. It drives some people to climb Mount Everest or the equally slippery corporate ladder. It drives others to teach, to perform research and even to write books. It is the engine of many of our disparate and desperate aspirations. Real self-esteem or self-acceptance is not based on the opinion of others but on 'real capacity, competence, and adequacy to the task', writes Maslow, and he warns that 'even here it is helpful to distinguish the actual competence and achievement that is based on sheer will power, determination and responsibility, from that which comes naturally and easily out of one's own true inner nature, one's constitution, one's biological fate or destiny, out of one's Real Self rather than out of the idealized pseudo-self'. At the highest level self-esteem comes very close to, and actually merges with, self-actualization.

Self–actualization

It would appear that if the needs so far discussed are met we would be satisfied – but very often a new need emerges, the need for self-actualization, or making one's potential actual. Maslow states: 'A musician must make music, an artist must paint, a poet must write if he is to be ultimately at peace within himself. What a man can be, he must be. He must be true to his own nature.'

Perhaps one of the great inadequacies of western society that it provides so well for our physiological and safety needs; it provides many opportunities for the satisfaction of our belonging needs and for acquiring status, somewhat fewer for self-esteem; but it does little to encourage self-actualization. The workplace actually discourages it, so self-actualization, if pursued at all, is seldom associated with a conventional commercial work environment. The need of self-actualizing people is to find meaning and purpose in their means of self-expression. This almost invariably includes contributing to others and to the larger whole.

Self-realization

There is one further state to which a few people aspire beyond self-actualization and which Maslow did not include in his diagram. It is called self-realization. If people find meaning and purpose in their personal life through self-actualization, they find meaning in the world we live in – ultimately the meaning of life itself – through self-realization. This is a rare state of grace and tranquillity so profound and experiential as to be almost indescribable.

It is essentially manifesting our deeper spiritual nature in every moment of our daily life. We will touch on this elevated state again in chapters 12 and 15, but for now we are going to take a look at how Maslow's model helps to clarify motivation in the workplace.

Management and motivation

From the above examination of the stages of Maslow's model, it is clear how the world of work serves to meet a number of our levels of need, theoretically at least enabling us to move on to the next need. If this too is met wholly or in part at work, we will be happy. To the extent that it is not, we will seek to meet that need outside the workplace. It surprises me that so few businesses take Maslow's hierarchy into account when they structure their methods of motivating staff and employees. They resort to other traditional methods of motivation as the best or the only ones available, without really thinking them through or recognizing that people's needs are changing, or should I say collectively evolving. What worked in the past may no longer be appropriate today.

Ever since work began, reward and punishment, some form of carrot and stick, have been used to motivate people. In our history books the stick was big and the carrots were small. The stick sometimes consisted of the threat of withholding the carrot. However, the reward was either food, the money to buy it or a plot of land on which to grow your own.

To make work attractive the size of the reward grew sufficiently to meet the needs for clothing and a roof under which to shelter. It was not so long ago that in Britain farm workers and those in some other industries were supplied with tied housing as an incentive. The very nature of most work brings people together and thereby meets some of the belonging need, provided that the place of work is pleasant enough for employees to want to belong. If it is not, but other work is scarce, the belonging need may be met by employees uniting against their common enemy, the employer. The growth of union movements all over the world met this need. A few more enlightened early industrialists, such as Robert Owen from Lanarkshire in Scotland, sought consciously to take care of all these needs by building a supportive community around the mills.

In rural Britain and in the industrial towns of the 19th century, workers knew their place and class barriers inhibited any expectations of promotion up the hierarchy. On one hand there was little chance for the need for status to be met, but in evolutionary terms workers were still focused on meeting the three lower levels of need.

Only during the 20th century and especially in the 50 years following the Second World War has the real possibility emerged for the majority of people to be able to climb the corporate or social ladder. Some don't want to, some don't succeed, some want to but don't try, and yet others do and achieve status and wealth beyond the dreams of their parents' generation. They tend to do this ostentatiously because they are meeting the need for recognition or status. Business offers opportunities to meet this need with promotion, grandiose titles that belie the mundanity of the job, awards given in front of their peers, better company cars than those of lesser mortals and mentions in the company journal.

As business and society have evolved, the needs and the rewards have roughly kept pace with each other, moving inexorably up

Maslow's hierarchy. It is reasonably possible at present within the traditional workplace structure at least partially to meet the first, second and third needs, and half of the fourth need, the need for status. At this point in the evolution of work motivators, the system breaks down.

The need which is now fast emerging for many working people is that for self-esteem, and here the traditional hierarchical structure of business and management fails abysmally. It is true that businesses have of late chosen or been forced to delayer or flatten their structure, but the concept of empowerment has been bandied about too much and debased by verbiage and inaction. Fundamental culture change is the stated goal of many boards of directors who barely understand what it means and would be scared of it if they did. These constitute signs that businesses are at least thinking of moving in the direction in which they have to go if they are to meet the growing self-esteem needs of their staff.

Real empowerment meets the need for self-esteem, whereas the illusion of it frustrates and demotivates. The title without the power of decision making that should accompany it may meet the need for status, but it damages self-esteem. Captains of industry talk a good empowerment game but don't empower others for fear of the loss of their own power. This fear is unwarranted, because in real empowerment there are no losers. The process of empowering others is outlined in chapter 6, and described more fully in my book *Coaching for Performance*.

Self-esteem brings with it self-motivation, which dramatically improves performance. Business managers talk about self-motivation, but usually as something that people either have or do not have rather than as something that can be generated. It can be. All of us can recall some unpaid task, even a dirty one, which we performed well, quickly, creatively, unswervingly, uninterrupted by unnecessary coffee breaks, simply because we passionately wanted to do it. If we applied that level of dedication to all our tasks at work, wouldn't our performance rise astronomically? This can only be brought about in the workplace by a fundamental change in management style, to one that is based on the principles of good coaching.

While more and more people are looking for ways to meet the

need for self-esteem but not finding it at work, they may seek it in their leisure pursuits, which may mean that effort and energy in the workplace decline, with a consequent drop in performance. Alternatively, they may focus on developing a plan to become self-employed and during this transition phase they may be serving their own needs better than those of their employer. So not only are many companies missing out on the opportunity to generate high levels of performance through having self-motivated staff, their failure to empower their employees may in fact result in a reduction in performance.

While many people reach the self-esteem point in their own evolution, others are less fortunate and may have been driven down the hierarchy of needs by redundancy, job insecurity or negative equity (where they owe more on their mortgage than their house is now worth). It is therefore essential to keep in place the traditional motivators such as pay, job security and promotion where possible, since the lower-level needs are still there, but the envelope of motivators must also be stretched upwards to include the higher needs.

Few people may be exclusively seeking to meet the very highest need, as all of us span several needs, if not all of them. If you are at the level of the highest need, it is unlikely that you will be working for the average corporate employer. You will almost certainly be working for a smaller company meeting a special social need, a charity or a public service institution. Why? Self-actualizers obviously need a certain income, but their material requirements are small and they are not motivated by money. They do not seek recognition or power for its own sake. Self-esteem is not an issue for them because they know who they are and they have nothing to prove to themselves or others. What they need is for their work and life to be meaningful.

While the search for meaning may take other forms such as creativity, it nearly always implies work that makes a genuine contribution to the greater whole. The greater whole again refers to all of humanity rather than to any particular company or organization. If a company is to retain such people, its purpose, products and services will have to improve the human condition and be ethical. It is not surprising that self-actualizers tend to desert the commercial rat race and choose to work for charities and the like or to become self-employed. It is also not surprising that the ethics of companies are coming under the scrutiny of the public and even of some of their staff. Social evolution has reached the point at which there is a felt need for value and ethics.

As discussed before, the process of achieving self-actualization is more obscure and convoluted than has been described here, but I have kept it simple for illustrative purposes. Future chapters will address coaching as a means of empowering, ethics in business and the progressive expansion of a person's area of concern.

Before doing so, however, we will take a trawl through the marketplace to see what is on offer, who buys it and why, from Maslow's point of view. We will also identify the real **need** of those in many parts of the world for whom the need for recognition would appear to be an unnecessary luxury, and one that is destined to remain out of reach. What, if any, responsibility either businesses or individuals take for helping to meet these needs will depend on where they stand on Maslow's hierarchy.

5
The Greed and the Need

The products and services that we demand and that business offers are directly related to our collective level of psychological evolution. In recent years consumerism and its suppliers have flourished, as we would expect at a time when the bulk of our society is busy meeting, or aspiring to meet, Maslow's need for status. This is, of course, the stuff of *assertion*. As humanity evolves towards a state of *cooperation*, business will have to begin to offer what more psychologically mature people want, rather than what less mature people can be persuaded to buy.

Paralleling the trend of employees to respond better to motivation methods which take account of their need to develop their self-esteem, consumers will begin to seek products and services which suit their self-esteem requirements. Self-esteem is built by expressing our potential, by 'knowing who we are', by being authentic with ourselves and one another; no longer by trying to prove anything to others but by being true to one's own best standards. Self-actualizing people take these principles still further. Ostentatious consumerism runs directly counter to their mentality, and while these changes will take their time collectively, and there will always be some people who are just reaching the status stage, more and more people are now aspiring to meet their self-esteem needs. It is inevitable that new products will appear and old industries will die unless their offerings become less superficial and more authentic and practical.

Spending for status

Let's take a look at how business currently profits from our collective *assertive* behaviour and our need for status. In the 1980s,

Thatcherism in the UK and Reaganism in the US made a virtue out of ostentatious displays of consumer spending, selfishness, winners and losers, excess and 'yuppie' values. The recession put paid to all that, and we are unlikely to revert to quite such a primitive state so readily in future. Thatcher and Reagan are no longer in power, but **greed** will remain with us for a while yet, for as long as it takes us to leave the *assertion* stage behind.

Fashion

Being *in* fashion is *inclusion* behaviour. Seeking *ex*clusivity through *ex*cessive *ex*penditure on fashion is *assertion* behaviour. *Cooperative* people are seldom concerned about either. In the very long term, the fashion business is probably doomed by evolution – as people develop, it will no longer have such a high status. However, for the time being it is a vast and lucrative industry preying on our collective psychological immaturity. Fashion designers, couturiers, boutiques, jewellers, fashion magazines and tabloid newspapers all conspire with our own egos to keep us buying.

I am all for excellence – but a great deal of fashion is rubbish. Designer jeans and 'grunge' were among the most preposterous and profitable of all mass-market fashion items in the 1990s. If you could sell your label at a premium on everyday working clothes, as Calvin Klein and Doc Martin did, or if you can turn trainers into fashion accessories that American delinquents will kill for, as Nike and Reebok have, you are on to a winner. If you can manufacture down-market goods using cheap labour, sell them at a huge mark-up as up-market products at up-market prices to gullible status seekers, you are on to a real winner. But what about the losers?

Sweatshops

There will always be winners in business but plenty of losers too, not only during a recession. Even in boom times there are losers, though they are less visible and vociferous, often hidden away in sweatshops far from the profit centres. Manufacturing is increasingly being transferred to the fast-developing countries of the Far East where wages are still comparatively low, the health and safety conditions in the factory fall far below minimum European standards and under-age

The world according to Nike.

children are employed for long hours at a pittance. If US and European companies knowingly condone or encourage working processes and practices that are illegal back home, they are guilty of culpable exploitation and a failure of ethics, irrespective of the willingness of the exploited to be used in this way.

In December 1995 the British Sunday newspaper the *Observer* reported that workers making Reebok, Nike and Adidas trainers in a stinking, noisy, overheated factory in Indonesia are paid 25 cents an hour – and that the wholesale price of a pair of Nike Air shoes that retail for $70 is $37.80, of which the total labour content is $1.66. Nike's profits then amounted to $300 million a year and they pay untold millions of dollars to sports stars to wear and endorse their products. Depending on your perspective, it is either smart, a pity or inexcusable that they don't pay their workers a little more of the spoils.

No one will deny that there is a great **need** for employment in many countries of the Far East, or that meeting that need by providing employment offers short-term financial benefits for some people in those countries. At first glance this seems to be a good thing. The populations of countries such as Hong Kong and Taiwan have in the past benefited hugely, in terms of their material standard of living, by manufacturing for the West. How long doing so will continue to provide an improvement in the quality of life for the workforce, and how equitably the cake is divided, are hard questions to answer. Will the same benefits accrue to Indonesia, the Philippines, Thailand and other countries on the next growth wave – or will the wave turn out to be a 'dumper'?

Designer labels

A few years ago a large business was uncovered in New York illegally producing indistinguishable replica designer-label jeans, T-shirts and other accessories, which it was selling at a fraction of the price of the real thing, but nevertheless at a nice profit. It is quite likely that some of the garments were made in the same factory in the Far East on the same production line as the 'real' thing. Paradoxically, the laws of our society hold the owners of this business to be criminals – though they were selling products for approximately what they were worth (a T-shirt is only a T-shirt after all) – while protecting the rights and excessive profits of the 'designers', who sell cheap wares at obscene prices.

Diamonds

At the other end of the monetary scale, perhaps the most durable *assertion* asset is the diamond. This pebble, no more attractive to the average punter than a chunk of shattered windscreen, has for centuries been the symbol of wealth and exclusivity for kings, princes, film stars and the *nouveau riche*. No wonder there was panic in 1992 when cheap gem diamonds from Angola, and cheap industrial diamonds from Russia, threatened the producers' prices, the monopoly of De Beers and the exclusivity of the diamond itself.

Is it just a coincidence that hippies, who made an exploratory foray into *cooperation* in the 1960s, did much to popularize the rock shops now to be found in most small towns and markets? Rocks, far more stunningly coloured and textured and far larger than diamonds, but at a fraction of the cost, are sought after by people who care more about natural beauty than exclusivity.

Furs

Fur coats are evidence of natural beauty too, but only when worn by their original owner. Some people will kill and steal the coat off the corpse's back to meet their need for status, or at least get someone else to do it for them for profit. A few decades ago no one thought twice about wearing fur if they had the chance, but we are gradually becoming more aware. We do something similar with cows, of course, for both shoes and food. It is just so much more distasteful when the animal is rare and wild, and when it is perpetrated for show rather than for basic foodstuffs; though I don't suppose that makes much difference to how the animal feels. Is mad cow disease the animals' revenge, and can we catch it from brogues as well as burgers?

Mobile status

But haven't we also turned our homes and our cars, intended for shelter and transport, into objects of fashion? We display them, we compare them to those possessed by others, we compete with each other for promotion and for the reward of a better company car. Cars are chosen more meticulously for the status they bestow than for their suitability for the task. For many people in the western world, the car is much more than a means of transport. Encouraged by our own egos, and seduced by the advertising of a flourishing industry, we have convinced ourselves that we need luxury and power, and so we have off-road vehicles that never go off the road, or 'people carriers' that never carry more than four of us.

We have convinced ourselves also that we need all manner of elec-tronic wizardry, mechanical gadgetry and aerodynamic wings and spoilers for our morning crawl to the office. All that junk might even be justifiable if it served some genuine function on the weekend drive in the country. However, that is a thing of the past – we are sick of, and from, driving by the end of the week; weekend traffic is even worse; restrictions and roadworks abound; and a pass or two up and down the lawn with the motor mower is the closest we are likely to get to the good old days of open-air motoring in the countryside.

So, on the one hand we covet and possess ever more sleek and potent projectiles; on the other hand the arena for play and display becomes more and more limited and overcrowded.

The conditions no longer exist, if indeed they ever did, for using a major, seemingly essential method of transport as a means of meeting our *assertion* and status needs, which range from machismo to the more subtle 'keeping up with the Joneses'. The car is the vehicle for this behaviour because it is the second most expensive item most of us own, and one which, unlike our house, we can show off all over the place. It is at once a measure of our wealth and success, a symbol of power and sex and an insulated mobile tank in which we can challenge and defeat our opponents on Status Street.

People who cannot afford a prestige car may customize a mundane model by altering its shape, its colour or its trim. More often they buy mass-produced exclusivity symbols from auto supermarkets, side flashes with the words 'special' or 'designer' or 'aristocrap' emblazoned for all to see. They adorn the car's exterior with expensive spoilers and wings, useless at less than 100mph, to give the impression of speed. Motor manufacturers have found it profitable to add to the illusion of exclusivity by offering limited editions of popular models. What these consist of, of course, is a standard car with a few accessories thrown in, a different wheel trim, a sexy label and a new price tag. So long as the seller sells another car, and the buyers can delude themselves and their neighbours that they are getting something better, everyone is happy.

Personalized or cherished number plates, as they are called, are seen as another ticket to the top drawer. At a recent auction some status freak paid over £230,000 for KI NGS, and now he can advertise his folly at both ends of his tin can. Hundreds of people pay thousands of pounds for misspelled names and words that are intended to single them out from the others who also possess a motley collection of letters and numbers. How silly can we human beings get?

It would seem much more sensible to save our lives, our environment and our money, by investing in effective mass transit systems and a little mass psychotherapy. However, there is a huge auto industry which thrives on our foibles, which does not want us to grow up and be sensible. And it spends a fortune persuading us that we need its seductive products. It wants to push us up-market, since there is more profit in a bigger, faster or more decorated wooshmobile than there is in a basic form of transport.

However, there are some good signs. The motor industry is alert to the gradually evolving consciousness of people who are beginning to spend more of their auto dollars on safety devices and less on decoration. We are using unleaded fuel. Motor manufacturers, partially

driven by environmental legislation, are more actively developing
alternative power sources. A proportion of some new cars have
already been recycled once and a larger percentage of new components are recyclable for the future. Even though cars are little by little
becoming more environmentally friendly, it can still be argued that
the manufacturing process of a car is more environmentally damaging than everything that comes out of its exhaust in its whole life. If
that is really so, we should buy only used cars, even if they are not fit-
ted with the latest ecogadget!

We have the design skills, the electronic ingenuity, the new materi-
als, the manufacturing capability, the workforce and the very real
need to develop new, comprehensive, integrated public and private
transport systems which meet environmental, flexibility, capacity, collective and individual requirements. We do not yet have the political
will or the personal motivation to act. When we have exhausted our
seemingly insatiable status needs, we will let go of our identification

and love affair with the sleek and shiny aspect of a noisy, smelly, dirty and dangerous lump of metal and plastic.

Status rules

Peculiar public automotive displays of vicarious self-importance are not restricted to otherwise obscure people. The Sultan of Brunei has more exclusive cars (including a couple of £1/2 million McLaren F1s, to which will soon be added a £300,000 Bentley convertible) and seemingly a greater status need than any ruler today. In fact, those cars constitute a very small part of his reputed personal fortune of £40 billion. Other toys have served a similar purpose. Imelda Marcos needed 900 pairs of shoes, Emperor Bokassa of the Central African Republic demanded the richest bejewelled throne in the world and some past and present members of the British royal family are not renowned for their frugality. The sale in 1996 of some of Jacqueline Kennedy Onassis's possessions for an unexpected fortune demonstrated the status-bestowing staying power of the last American royal family.

The irony is that if we ourselves are in the *inclusion* stage we want our leaders and heroes to be special, different and on a rich pedestal. In our *assertion* stage we challenge them and want the pedestal for ourselves. In the *cooperation* stage we want them to come down and be normal human beings like the rest of us, which is all they really are. This was exemplified by the British royals who in recent years have gone through a series of very public marital crises: some people felt let down because they were no longer special (*inclusion* stage); others put them down for being inadequate (*assertion* stage); and yet others were relieved that they were beginning to show that they were normal (*cooperation* stage).

Static status

There is a small town in Northern Italy called San Gimignano, which from a distance resembles a cluster of tall, chimneyed factories. Sprouting from the roofs of many of its houses are very tall and precarious-looking watch towers. In an earlier century in that town, the height of one's tower was considered to be the symbol of one's wealth and status. The competition was fierce, the stakes were high and the accidents frequent. And the idea was not exclusive to Italy. English feudal barons jousted with the splendour of their castles, and stately homes sprouted up to overshadow one another for much the same reason and in much the same way as stockbrokers keep up with the Joneses in Surrey today. The *assertion* game is alive and well in the shires.

Some 20 years ago I stayed in a hotel near San Francisco airport that was all front and no substance. It was hideous: the polystyrene façade of a Norman castle was incongruously topped with phoney Tudor architecture, complete with imitation beams. Inside family portraits moulded in one-piece plastic, frame and all, shared the walls with glassfibre suits of armour and toy swords and spears. Maybe one day the good taste police will have it demolished.

I reminded myself at the time that I was in the land of Hollywood make-believe, hungry for the antiquity of Europe, and that we British would never do that. I was wrong. Today, if one's home is too bland to earn one the respect of neighbours and passers-by, one can acquire from the DIY superstore down the road all manner of alternative façades and mouldings mass produced out of polystyrene for foolproof fitting and instant exclusivity. Very few of us are immune to the tempting array of 'instant home improvement opportunities'; and big home improvement stores have become even bigger business. At least the fake French shutters which I bought to improve the appearance of our house were made of wood!

Dental gloss

It is not only large or expensive items like furs and fashion accessories, cars and castles with which we play the *assertion* game, and from which business profits so much.

Take the humble toothbrush, for example. Having a better brush and renewing it frequently is what the £100 million British toothbrush industry recommends. There is, however, no evidence that any of the heavily promoted longer, rounder, smoother, sharper, straighter, more flexible sculptured bristles or handles do anything at all for dental hygiene, nor do they wear out in three months as the industry claims. There is a lot of evidence that these claims compel us to purchase the latest one, and frequently, and enable the manufacturers to hike up the price. 'My toothbrush is better and newer than yours!' A toothbrush costs about 10p to make, but its average selling price in 1996 of £1.50 is more than twice what it was in 1991. For a piece of plastic with a tuft on the end, that is quite a rip-off – but nothing when compared to designer spectacle frames at £60 and more, just another piece of plastic but without the tuft!

The esteem of others is either earned honestly and not directly sought, or it is undeservedly obtained by conning others with the baubles that we were conned to buy in the first place. Maintaining that charade is hard. Conning is bad for relationships and for business, and few things damage our self-esteem more. In the coming years the commercial importance of status will gradually be eroded by the self-esteem factor, and businesses will need to stop playing on the gullibility of their punters and begin to offer more honest products and services to meet the changing needs and values of more discerning customers.

The need

Assertion and status seeking cause such crazy behaviour, but behaviour that we all peform to some extent, however covertly, that we really need to laugh at ourselves. And business laughs all the way to the overstuffed bank. There is a more serious side to this, though. The problem with the *assertion* game is that wherever there are winners, there are also losers. In a society which is predominantly in its *assertion* stage, as our western society is, the winners get richer at the expense of the poor, who may be left struggling for mere *inclusion*. We have neither sufficient capacity for caring nor the collective will to act for the common good. We continue to exercise our power over the less assertive by manipulating the game that we control for our own advantage. We flaunt our possessions and we *assert* our power with crude displays of both. The more we have, the more we want. Our hunger for the esteem of others seems never to be satisfied – and neither is the real hunger of those we could feed, but don't.

Felt need

We have all experienced the need for *inclusion*, the need to belong, and also the emotional security of being with a close family or others of like mind, of being a part of a group. At times we are also likely to have felt alone, isolated, misunderstood or excluded, feelings reminiscent of childhood vulnerability. This is the level at which our western society enters the system and where our three-stage model rises in parallel with Maslow's hierarchy. In the context of the title of this book, the level of belonging is one of **need** – but much of the world's population would be extremely grateful just to get to our level. Too many people are condemned to a life of struggle to meet their most basic needs.

We in the so-called developed world have virtually no understanding of what it feels like to live continuously in **need**. Other than in exceptional circumstances, our needs for food and water, sex and a roof over our head have seldom been seriously at risk. Even so, in Britain in the mid-1990s concerns about the basic needs have returned: one-fifth of the population of Britain lives below the poverty line, and a large number of families have the constant worry of losing their home. Paying the mortgage has become a real trial for them. Because basic needs are so fundamental to our instinct for survival, we are never totally free of concern about them, however unjustified that concern may be. There is a barely distinguishable difference for us between *feeling* emotionally insecure and actually *being* that way. Felt needs are real needs, however unreal they may appear from the perspective of another with a greater degree of need.

Poverty

Communism has proved to be a failure – but let's not delude ourselves, so has capitalism. The capitalist ideals of Adam Smith have failed to deliver, nationally or globally, the promise of trickling down wealth to all. Throughout the world the rich are getting richer and the poor are getting poorer. For example, in 1991 the poorer countries of the South paid $20 billion more in loan interest and capital repayments to the rich countries of the North than they received from them in new loans and investments. The world aid total in that year was $50 billion, which is only a third of the amount these countries are estimated to lose through unfair trade. The cycle of crises continues.

There is no doubt about the reality of the **needs** of literally billions of people in the developing world, especially and tragically as so many of them are children. In 1995 700 million people went to bed every night chronically ill with malnutrition and 18 million people died of hunger, more than half of whom were children. Events in the 1990s have focused our attention on Africa, but starvation, utter deprivation, fear, desperate need and little children are on the streets on every continent, including Europe and North America. These people are struggling to meet the most basic level of physical survival. *Inclusion* is not yet their concern, but if it was, what hope do they have of meeting that need if they are stateless or homeless, refugees or orphans?

The majority of us have acquired the technology that enables us to look at moving pictures of the poor and the suffering whenever we want to from the warmth of our homes. All too often we choose not to, because it makes our comfort uncomfortable. We switch channels. The vast amount that has been spent on developing television and entertaining us all with it would have been sufficient to supply everyone in the world with food, shelter, clean water and basic healthcare for the foreseeable future. Wouldn't that have been a better investment? Perhaps seeing the horrors on television is an essential step to get us to take global action to meet the very real **needs** of which we can no longer claim ignorance. Our current choice is simply to go on pushing another button to give us simulated sex and violence, or a good laugh when we get bored of the reality, or when it makes us feel sick, guilty or powerless.

Biafra, Bangladesh, Ethiopia, Somalia, Rwanda, Romania and Bosnia. Each brought a spontaneous outpouring of public generosity, but if it was not too little and too late to solve the immediate crisis, it certainly was too late to prevent the crisis arising in the first place. Disasters are only reported on television once they have happened, and it is already too late. Many are preventable and most are predictable, but the collective will of the public, governments and those who control the world's resources just is not there.

One of the problems of television is that it focuses public attention on to a new and captivating crisis, while other less dramatic but ongoing, festering problem areas are overshadowed. Once the most prominent problem is solved, we tend to sit back and feel that we have done our bit until the next one occurs. The permanent tragedies are not news, and are not noticed.

I travelled on an early relief flight into the newly liberated Romania a few years ago. The most memorable incident of the trip for me was a comment made by an intense young woman as she surveyed the boxes of medical supplies. She said, 'We are grateful for what you are bringing us today, but our real needs are only just beginning. This mess will take ten years to clean up and you will have forgotten us and be looking elsewhere in nine months' time when we will need you most.' How profoundly true that turned out to be.

The permanent resolution of mass starvation, basic global health-care, clean water for all, the preservation and equitable sharing of the world's resources are all possible now, and yet they have hardly begun. Of course we nibble around the edges, a small but growing band of people give their lives to, and sometimes for, the suffering of others, great events like Live Aid pluck at our heart and our purse strings, and governments and the World Bank give grants, but too often for ill-conceived projects and with other strings attached. Overall the problems are still getting worse.

On aid issues at least, First World governments are weak, ineffective and devoid of vision. Even if they were motivated to address the global deprivation of basic **needs**, they would achieve little. Only Sweden among the developed nations has honoured the pledge made to the UN to provide aid amounting to just 1 per cent of GNP. It is within the power and in the long-term interest of business to take responsibility and be responsive to the very real **needs** that abound and surround us now. This can only be achieved collectively by setting aside the barriers of commercial mistrust and protectiveness and by *cooperation* between corporations, aid agencies and governments; something that at present seems regrettably remote and utopian.

All of us seem to be stuck. *They* are overwhelmed by **need**, and *we* are overwhelmed with **greed**. **Need** and **greed** go hand in hand. So long as **greed** exists, there will always be **need**. So long as I have *more* than I need, other people will have *less* than they need. **Freedom** from **need** and from **greed** is the next giant step for humanity.

Theirs is the need for food, drink and shelter, and to struggle for inclusion.

For us it is greed, giving up status and the need for assertion.

When freedom from the need and the greed means cooperation, there will be no separation between them and us.

6
Business Team Leadership

Leadership in business calls for vision and inspiration, and for a great deal more besides. It is the subject of many books and workshops, and of some controversy. And traditional hierarchical leadership is in terminal decline, though it is by no means dead. The views and past achievements of dominant, autocratic leaders go against the expectations of today's workforce, who want more democracy.

Assertion is the name of the business game. Competition is at the heart of the capitalist ethic. The structures of business, manufacturing, service and financial industries foster and have thrived on *assertive* behaviour.

But there are signs that *assertive* behaviour is not the panacea it once was. Higher performance levels are constantly being demanded of fewer people. Individual performance-related pay, the very stuff of *assertion*, has not delivered its promises. Team performance pay is more *cooperative* and more promising. To attract and hold on to the best staff, attention is being paid by the most progressive companies to improving the quality of life in the workplace.

The traditional command-and-control style of management works well enough with teams in their *inclusion* stage. It works sufficiently well to keep control in the turbulent *assertive* stage of a team. However, as soon as a team is expected to go beyond that to become *cooperative*, dictating is no longer feasible. Coaching, or at least a management style which is based on the same underlying principles, is imperative. By its very nature coaching is *cooperative* rather than *assertive*, and it is widely seen as the most effective management style of the truly participative and productive team.

Coaching

What do we mean by coaching? Its purpose is to unlock a person's or a team's potential to optimize their performance. It presupposes that everyone has more potential within than they currently deliver. It recognizes, however, that there are personal and cultural, internal and external, and historical and immediate factors that inhibit performance. Coaching achieves its objective by reducing and eliminating these barriers, and by proactively fostering the energy, creativity, self-esteem, self-motivation and vision which are then released.

Coaching is a facilitative process which in the main employs questions as opposed to statements or commands. Questions cause people to think for themselves, allowing better recall, self-reliance, self-esteem and personal choice, and the answers received provide a feedback loop. The specific object of the questions is to raise the performer's <u>awareness</u> and <u>responsibility</u>. These are the two indispensable qualities that are key to performance, learning and enjoyment at work or at play. The words are commonplace, but their true meaning is poorly understood.

Awareness

Increased <u>awareness</u> provides people with a higher quality and quantity of input on which to base their actions. I use the term input rather than information because we tend to think of information as something obtained exclusively from an external source, whereas input can be gathered in a variety of ways, including from our senses, by observation, by deduction, by creative contemplation, by experimentation and by experience. This suggests that the answers are often within us if only we knew how and where to look. The questions invite and facilitate the looking.

I can illustrate both the effect of the right question and the higher quality of <u>awareness</u> obtained by a very simple example from sport, from tennis in particular. The most basic and common instruction in all ball sports is 'Keep your eye on the ball'. It is indeed the single most important thing to do. However, in the main the instruction to do this does not cause a tennis player to watch the ball. Consider for a moment which of the following phrases is most likely to make you watch the ball:

❑ Watch the ball.
❑ Are you watching the ball?
❑ Which way is the ball spinning?

Most people immediately recognize that the third one would be the most effective. We might then ask what all those tennis coaches – or should we say instructors – are doing out there telling their clients to watch the ball.

When people really do watch the ball the improvement in performance can be remarkable. But why specifically does the third question work? Neither of the others provides any verifiable feedback to the coach. The answer given to 'Are you watching the ball?' will invariably be 'yes', whether or not this is the case, but so what? We are back to square one.

On the other hand, it is impossible to give an answer to 'Which way is the ball spinning?' without seeing the ball. The coach now has feedback and can verify what the player is seeing. The player has to focus more acutely to see the fine detail of the spin of the ball, which results in higher than normal input about its precise trajectory. The result is improved output in terms of a centred hit, a more accurate shot and a correspondingly higher performance.

That was the proactive part, but what were the performance-inhibiting factors that were eliminated at the same time? The high-quality, focused attention on the ball is so all-consuming that it excludes a myriad of distracting and disruptive factors. The presence of external distractions such as noise and movement on surrounding courts is obvious, but the power of internal factors such as fear of failure, self-instruction and self-criticism, which create tension and inhibit movement, is less well recognized. These distractions are swept aside when a player is truly watching the spin of the ball.

It requires no great leap to transpose that analogy into a wide variety of far more complex situations in the workplace. After attending a coaching course with me, one senior manager suggested supplying every course participant with a tennis ball on which was printed, 'Which way is the ball spinning in your department?'. Coaching has a great potential for performance improvement at work through higher-quality input and the elimination of distraction alone – but that is only the <u>awareness</u> part, what about <u>responsibility</u>?

Responsibility

'You are responsible for…' is not an uncommon statement or command in the workplace, but does it produce the desired result? All it does is identify someone to blame when things go wrong. Another analogy illustrates a better way, this time from the field of work.

> As the foreman of a firm of builders and decorators, I tell one of my men, Fred, to 'Go and get a ladder. There is one in the shed.' What will he do if he finds no ladder in the shed? He will probably come back and say, 'No ladder, guv.' I could have used a different approach and asked my men, 'Who is going to get me a ladder? There is one in the shed.' Let's say that Fred responds, 'I will handle that.' Off he goes, but again there is no ladder in the shed. What will he do this time? The chances are that he will go and look elsewhere until he finds one. Why?
>
> In both cases Fred arrives at the shed with the same intention. But when he sees there is no ladder, his behaviour is different. In the second case he looks elsewhere for a ladder because I have offered him <u>responsibility</u> and he has chosen to accept it. He is, in part at least, now doing it for himself. I introduced self-motivation, which results in an altogether higher level of commitment and performance, and so he comes back with a ladder. What did I do differently? I asked him a question and heard his response instead of giving him a command.

Choice

The key to self-motivation is choice. Although we cannot always dole out tasks by choice, it is far more available than we think.

For example, some of our client companies 'send' participants to the courses we run, others offer them the choice of going. Those who are sent invariably are more resistant to the programme at the beginning. They have not chosen to be there. I point out to them that by being at the course, they have already met their obligation to the person who sent them, and that now they have another choice, the choice of how they wish to treat the course. They can do anything they want, from participating enthusiastically to merely regarding it as a break from work. When given this choice, which they always had but did not know it, any resistance tends to melt away.

Offering choice provides other benefits too. It encourages people to do things in their own preferred style, technique or sequence within the confines of the agreed goal. This allows them to employ and optimize their own unique combination of qualities to achieve the best result. Being trusted with making choices and being encouraged to use our own skills are crucial to building that vital quality, self-esteem, which leads to confidence, self-reliance and self-motivation.

The key to coaching is the recognition of the immense value of awareness and responsibility for generating performance, which I hope these examples illustrate. We only have to think of our own team at work to realize how productive it would be if its members were highly aware and highly responsible. Which questions are effective and which are not, and how and when to ask them, are elaborated in my book *Coaching for Performance*. That book also illustrates why and how coaching plays such a central role in the major culture change through which businesses will have to go to succeed in the 21st century.

Beyond the boundaries of business, however, awareness and responsibility are attitudinal keys to human and social development. While they are certainly not a panacea to all ills, by extrapolation they may be essential for planetary survival, a point that will be explained in future chapters. They certainly play a significant role in team building and teamworking in business.

We will now take a look at the function and management style of business team leaders who view their teams with an understanding of the three stages of team development.

The *inclusion* stage

Coaching models the qualities we would expect to see in a *cooperative* team. It encourages trust, support, openness, honesty, appreciation of differences, inclusiveness. In demonstrating these qualities by coaching individual team members and the team as a whole, the team leader is in effect saying, 'These are the values that I value.' It is especially important for a team leader to model these qualities him or herself, from the moment a new team comes together. At that time the team members are seeking to be *included* and accepted and they will conform to what they perceive as the group norms. To whom will they look first to be their role model? To the team leader.

By being open and disclosing a weakness or two of their own, team leaders can in effect say, 'Openness is one of the standards of this team' and 'It is OK to have and to admit to weaknesses here'. They can thereby introduce, demonstrate and establish at the outset some of the values of the *cooperation* stage which they hope the team will later reach. The team's evolutionary journey will be made easier because fewer adjustments will have to be made to values and behaviour along the way.

As well as encouraging *cooperative* qualities and behaviours, team coaches or leaders must fully recognize the real needs for *inclusion* and *assertion* within the team. These needs cannot be bypassed, glossed over, trivialized or avoided. They must be met to allow the individuals and the team to evolve to higher levels. A good team leader will be aware of the kind of *inclusion* concerns which the members of his new team are likely to have, look out for them and be prepared to address them creatively. It is no good simply doing with the new team what worked with the last one. Every team is made up of a unique mix of personalities.

Dr Meredith Belbin provided us with an excellent model which identifies eight different personality types, such as Completer/finishers and Shapers, and suggests that a balanced mix of these is ideal in a team. This model is helpful for the understanding of roles and functions, and with the need to cover missing elements, but that is by no means the complete picture; and most managers do not have the luxury of being able to select their team on those criteria.

Goals

One of the most important areas that a team leader needs to address to reduce the uncertainty associated with the *inclusion* stage is the understanding of the team's purpose and goals. Most new members will have arrived with some idea of the function of the team, but assumptions can not be made as interpretations may differ widely. A good place to start would be for the team leader to ask each team member to reflect on their understanding of the purpose and goals of the team, to try to define them in a sentence or two and then to share them with the others. The leader should participate in this and may bring in some elements of which the other team members were unaware. A composite definition can then be formed, which may be modified as time goes on. Every team member needs to have had the opportunity to have some input into that definition if they are to gain some sense of ownership of the team. At this early stage they should also be encouraged to share their personal aspirations for their participation in the team. Elements of this might be incorporated into the collective team goal definition, and everyone will have the opportunity to support each other in achieving their personal goals.

Roles

Roles are no less important than goals. When people are assigned a clear role, or whenever possible coached to define their own role, which is then affirmed by the team leader, they automatically feel included, they feel that they matter. In contrast, having a probationary period before the role is confirmed creates suspense and is anathema to *inclusion*. The act of coaching itself helps in *inclusion*: coaching is based on questioning and when a more senior person asks a subordinate a question, the covert message is 'I value your opinion or I would not ask for it'. But coaching must be authentic, and the answers must be heard. The most effective way to coach, and to demonstrate that you are hearing, is to base your next question on the answer to the last. Pre-prepared questions are to be avoided.

The leader must give attention to those who may feel insecure in the team because of unconfirmed selection, ill-defined roles, shyness or the quick formation of subgroups which deliberately or unintentionally exclude them. Team members most likely to feel or to be excluded are those who are in any way different to the others in personality, skill, role or even personal appearance. They are not accepted because they do not conform to the group norms. Good coaches will challenge the excluders to find ways to *include* the excluded, and will personally demonstrate their *inclusion* of everyone without appearing to favour any one person. Above all, anyone who feels excluded must be encouraged to feel safe enough to bring their feelings about it to the team leader and, better still, to the team. The team leader is not expected to have all the answers, but skilful listening and questioning will help team members to find their own best way forward.

Process

Team process meetings at which *inclusion*-related topics are discussed help to dispel fears. Process meetings do not deal with the team task but air the way in which the team will work, roles, communication, frequency of meetings, as well as individual hopes and aspirations. At such meetings each person should be encouraged to speak and give input equally, and to share any anxieties they might have about being a member of the team. Those who tend to dominate need to be reined in so that the less vociferous are not inhibited.

Something else which I have found most helpful for getting team members to settle down is to share with them a simple version of the three-stage model. They will then be less confused and threatened when they experience *inclusion* fears or *assertive* behaviour which is out of character, and it will help them to understand and make greater allowances for the behaviour of others during the early life of the team.

During the *inclusion* stage the team leader will probably experience the team as compliant, conforming and by and large *cooperative*. He or she may be feeling relieved and could become complacent, believing that this is going to be an easy team. The team members may even give the impression of being very *cooperative*, because the behaviours associated with conformity and *cooperation* are very similar. The difference, however, lies in the motive. People conform for their own good, but they *cooperate* for the good of the whole. This does not constitute a problem until or unless the interests of the individual differ from those of the team as a whole – and they often do!

The *assertion* stage

Team leaders will know that the honeymoon is over when the first challenge to their authority comes from a team member. Team members who were previously easy going may now begin confronting each other, and even the leader, causing minor feuds and appearing to argue for the sake of arguing rather than over anything substantive. They are, of course, arguing for the sake of *assertion*. Blaming others, name calling and put-downs become rife, and there is an abundance of statements like 'That's not my job', 'Who does he think he is?', 'She is encroaching on my space', 'You always/never do...' and 'Why the hell don't you...?'. Of course it is by no means always this bad, but it is better to be prepared.

Team leaders must not allow things to get out of control at this point. They may need to reassert their authority to meet the challenge, but not in a way that denies the right to challenge. They must listen to the content of the challenge and address that, even though they may know that the challenge itself is more relevant than the content. They may want to adopt a coaching style, but the now unruly team may be inviting a more autocratic response; retaining balance is important.

Business team leaders might even be tempted to react to signs of *assertive* behaviour by firing the first offender. However, this would only plunge the team back into the *inclusion* stage and the process of team development would be set back to the beginning again. By repeating this pattern, often quite unconsciously, the team leader maintains power and control but the team never develops.

Conflict and stress
Assertive behaviour and competitiveness between team members striving for esteem and self-esteem are the causes of much conflict, confusion and chaos. They may also result in exceptional levels of individual performance, but these in turn may be accompanied by high

stress and burn-out. Because performance is motivated by individual needs rather than by a wish for the success of the whole, the team's collective effectiveness may not benefit to anything like the same extent. Similar to what happens in the *inclusion* stage, decisions and choices, while able to be rationalized as being for the good of the team, are often geared more to the enhancement of the individual's reputation or position in the team than to the team's overall performance.

Team leaders now have a fine line to walk. They must not allow themselves to be cowed by this assertiveness or attempt to crush it, since within it lie energy, drive, creativity and competitiveness which need to be tempered and refined. They have to ride the storm by keeping a firm grip on the helm, but allowing the boat to find its own balance through the waves. A sense of direction is maintained, the risk of damage is reduced and the calmer waters of the *cooperation* stage are reached.

Throughout the *assertion* stage team leaders must value and give time to the team process. They must keep the lines of communication wide open. Most importantly, they must continue to model the qualities of the emerging *cooperation* stage, even when some team members may be exhibiting extreme *assertion*. The temptation to meet *assertion* with *assertion* may at times be high, but there is almost always a better way. The exercise of power is often the resort of those who doubt their own power – true power resides with those who use it wisely and sparingly.

The *cooperation* stage

The values and principles of *cooperation* are diametrically opposite to those of *assertion*. For business people who have played the *assertion* game all their working life, the values of *cooperation* may seem soft, strange and risky. Some of them are listed opposite.

These are just a few of the opposites that I identify with. You might disagree with some of them. We could each come up with a different list of qualities, along with some different opposites, but the list above is sufficient to give a clear indication of how difficult it is suddenly to abandon one set of values and behaviours in favour of the other.

Assertion	Cooperation
Command	Coach
Exclusive	Inclusive
Analysis	Synthesis
Divisive	Cohesive
Direction	Coordination
Independence	Interdependence
Thinking	Feeling
Promotion	Attraction
Suspicion	Trust
Take advantage	Support
Withholding	Openness
Expediency	Honesty
Advantage	Fairness
Hierarchy	Teams
Material values	Human values
Appearances	Truth
Closed	Sharing
Sees others as opponents	Sees others as partners
Concern for self	Concern for society
Masculine qualities	Feminine qualities
Will	Love

It would be impossible not to notice the parallels between the qualities of *assertion* and typical male attitudes and behaviour, and between the qualities of *cooperation* and those normally attributed to women. This is a minefield that I am ill equipped to enter, and I will not attempt to do so in this book, but I believe that it is of great significance today. The rise of women in business throughout society is both a reflection of and a prerequisite to the transformation of business culture and of society as a whole towards *cooperation*.

Some women, like Margaret Thatcher and some militant feminists, have understandably adopted male characteristics in order to break into the man's world. When the change comes, I hope they will revert or they will find themselves being part of the male problem, rather than part of the female solution! Our society as a whole and the business culture in particular need women and feminine attributes if they are to undergo the fundamental and necessary change from *assertion* to *cooperation*.

Letting go

For most business team leaders, the *cooperation* stage is something of which they may speak, but have little experience. Letting go of control may be the last thing on their mind, especially if they had a rough ride in the *assertion* stage, but that is just what they have to do. 'When you are willing to let go of control is the moment you finally gain control,' is an expression that all good skiers well understand. It is easier to say than to do, but the flow that accompanies release is magic. Business team leaders could learn a lot on the ski slopes, such as *cooperating* with gravity instead of resisting it or trying to dominate it! A light, sensitive, attentive and responsive touch is needed to run a *cooperative* business team.

A flow is a good way to describe the progress of a *cooperative* team, and it needs leadership to maintain the flow. Leaders cannot afford simply to sit back and do nothing at this stage, but what they should do is more like trim tabbing than making coarse course changes. The process time, opportunities for social contact, composition of the team, <u>awareness</u>, <u>responsibility</u> and goal clarity of the team all require maintenance. However, leaders should by now be sufficiently liberated from the day-to-day operations of the team to concentrate on the wider, more visionary and long-term issues of the business. The constant firefighting which besets most managers is, for the time being anyway, behind them.

However, any change of goal or personnel or other unexpected external factors can re-energize insecurities which could drive the team back down into *assertion* or even *inclusion* behaviours. This kind of change needs to be discussed by the team the instant it arises to minimize its impact. Another difficulty is always present. Since most business teams rarely achieve the *cooperation* stage, any team which does is something of an oddity, and so may feel isolated, insular and elitist. This danger will remain so long as *assertion* remains the norm.

Team development

There are few business people who have not come across the team development model identified by the words forming, storming, norming and performing. The parallels are probably obvious already, but certainly will become more so as we go through the business application of our three-stage model which embraces both norming and performing in the *cooperation* stage. Another equivalent four-stage model is described by Rupert Eales-White of Sundridge Park Management Centre as confusion, conflict, cooperation and commitment.

In 1990 Roger Harrison, a pioneer of organizational development, described three levels of consciousness in organizations, which correspond very closely to our three-stage model (figure 4).

Tables 1–4 outline how the three organizational types display their consciousness, their organizational philosophy, their attitude to change and how they manage change.

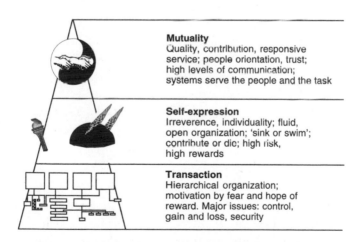

Mutuality
Quality, contribution, responsive service; people orientation, trust; high levels of communication; systems serve the people and the task

Self-expression
Irreverence, individuality; fluid, open organization; 'sink or swim'; contribute or die; high risk, high rewards

Transaction
Hierarchical organization; motivation by fear and hope of reward. Major issues: control, gain and loss, security

Figure 4: Three levels of consciousness in organizations

Table 1: Three levels of organizational consciousness

Transactional culture	Self-expression culture	Mutuality culture
Hierarchical, authoritarian	Autonomous, egalitarian	Affiliative, cooperative
Oriented to advantage, gain and profit	Oriented to achievement, impact, image	Oriented to responsive service, relationships
Reactive rather than initiating	Experimental, risk taking, proactive	Thoughtful, reflective, participative
Internally and externally exploitative	Aggressive in pursuit of success symbols	Seeking wholeness, integration
Competitive around power, status, rewards	Competitive on achievement	Cooperative and giving
Motivation by fear and hope of reward	Motivation to over-come obstacles, to succeed	Motivation to give and serve

Table 2: Organizational philosophies in three levels of organizational consciousness

Transactional culture	Self-expression culture	Mutuality culture
Invest in technology	Invest in people	Invest in teams
Technology and systems make up for deficiencies in people. They permit lower levels of mental functioning	Motivated, creative people make up for deficiencies in systems	Systems empower people and require learning to operate at higher levels of mental functioning
Technology as master	Technology as tools	Technology as servant
Strategy as the search for *advantage*	Strategy as the search for *excellence*	Strategy as the discovery and creation of *meaning* and *values*
Power as competitive edge	Speed and thrust as competitive edge	Wholeness, trust and cooperation as competitive edge

**Table 3: Thinking about change in three levels of
organizational consciousness**

Transactional culture	Self-expression culture	Mutuality culture
Dependency:	*Alignment:*	*Attunement:*
Identified with comfort, power, wealth	Identified with purpose, goals, achievements	Identified with harmonious growth
Disempowered – pawns of change	Empowered – origins of change	Related – interdependent change
Means oriented: organization as machine	Goal oriented: organization as purposeful entity	Systems oriented: organization as organism
Concrete: *things* are real	Creative: *ideas* are real	Systems thinking: *relationships* are real
Changer/changed: boss/subordinate	Changer/changed: leader/followers	Changer/changed: we/us

Table 4: Managing change at three levels of organizational evolution

Transactional culture	Self-expression culture	Mutuality culture
Sanction from hierarchy or system	Self-sanction by autonomous groups and individuals	Sanction through shared purpose and meaning
When authority speaks, there is surface compliance	Innovations must be sold locally	Consensus is slow, but commitment is high
Consultant as doer	Consultant as catalyst	Consultant as partner
Change is feared and often brutally imposed	Change may be sought for its novelty	Change is thoughtfully and compassionately undertaken
Participation is countercultural; authority is feared	Participation is demanded; conflict is high	Participation is normal; high value on agreement

By 1993 Harrison had added a fourth type of organizational culture which he saw more in parallel to or as an alternative to mutuality. His model became transactional, self-expression, mutuality and alignment. (You may remember this and the other models mentioned above from figure 1 in chapter 2.) Harrison described the first two stages as gratification driven and the second two as value driven (*see* figure 5), which can be equated with our spectrum of the driving impulse running from **need** at one end to **freedom** at the other.

At the same time Harrison developed another, all-encompassing model. 'The more elaborate and more complex model,' he wrote,

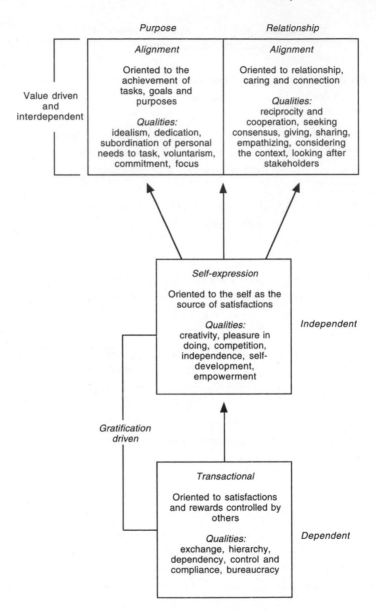

Figure 5: Four organization cultures

'satisfies my need for completeness and elegance, and it stimulates the interests of more theoretically minded colleagues.' He identified five levels of organizational consciousness: survival, defence, security, self-expression and transcendence (*see* figure 6).

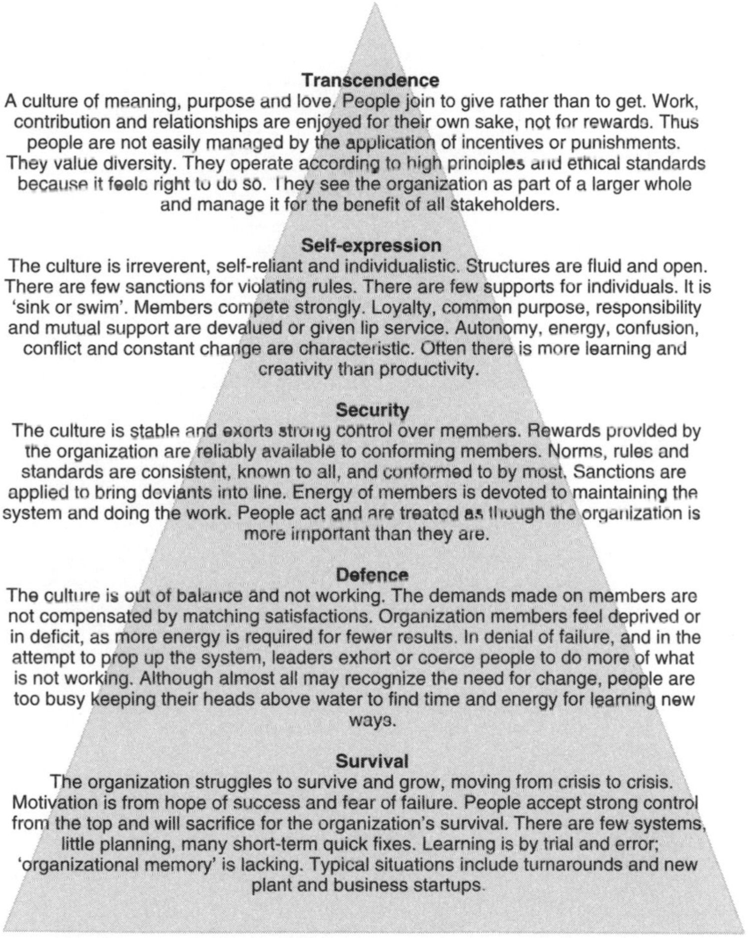

Transcendence
A culture of meaning, purpose and love. People join to give rather than to get. Work, contribution and relationships are enjoyed for their own sake, not for rewards. Thus people are not easily managed by the application of incentives or punishments. They value diversity. They operate according to high principles and ethical standards because it feels right to do so. They see the organization as part of a larger whole and manage it for the benefit of all stakeholders.

Self-expression
The culture is irreverent, self-reliant and individualistic. Structures are fluid and open. There are few sanctions for violating rules. There are few supports for individuals. It is 'sink or swim'. Members compete strongly. Loyalty, common purpose, responsibility and mutual support are devalued or given lip service. Autonomy, energy, confusion, conflict and constant change are characteristic. Often there is more learning and creativity than productivity.

Security
The culture is stable and exerts strong control over members. Rewards provided by the organization are reliably available to conforming members. Norms, rules and standards are consistent, known to all, and conformed to by most. Sanctions are applied to bring deviants into line. Energy of members is devoted to maintaining the system and doing the work. People act and are treated as though the organization is more important than they are.

Defence
The culture is out of balance and not working. The demands made on members are not compensated by matching satisfactions. Organization members feel deprived or in deficit, as more energy is required for fewer results. In denial of failure, and in the attempt to prop up the system, leaders exhort or coerce people to do more of what is not working. Although almost all may recognize the need for change, people are too busy keeping their heads above water to find time and energy for learning new ways.

Survival
The organization struggles to survive and grow, moving from crisis to crisis. Motivation is from hope of success and fear of failure. People accept strong control from the top and will sacrifice for the organization's survival. There are few systems, little planning, many short-term quick fixes. Learning is by trial and error; 'organizational memory' is lacking. Typical situations include turnarounds and new plant and business startups.

Figure 6: Overview of five levels of organizational consciousness

In 1953 McClelland had identified human needs and motives under three headings: power, achievement and affiliation. To these Harrison added a fourth domain, form, as a central feature of organizational consciousness. He now superimposed over each domain the five levels of organizational consciousness, to come up with his complete model. In figure 7 I have included a word to qualify the predominant attitudes or behaviours in each of the segments.

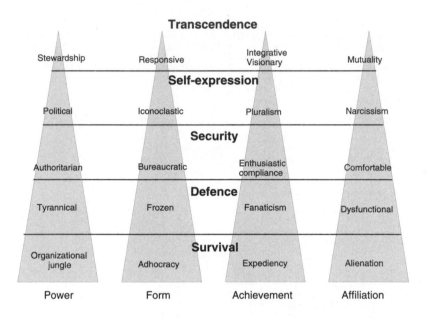

**Figure 7: Five levels of organizational consciousness
in four domains of organizational culture**

For a full description of this model, I highly recommend *The Collected Papers of Roger Harrison* (McGraw-Hill 1995). In it Harrison tells how he wrestled with the integration of Maslow's hierarchy and other organizational development models from his own experience and of his own creation. By 1994 he had produced what is in my opinion a highly sophisticated model which has tremendous value for the thorough examination, understanding, diagnosis and healing of any organization.

Back to simplicity

For the purpose of this book, however, which is to provide a map which is simple and easy to understand and one which applies equally well to all forms of social structure, I have chosen to stick with our straightforward three-stage model as applied to business – and to everything else! To propel or rather progress a business team quickly and smoothly upwards through the first two stages of development to attain *cooperation* should be the goal of any team leader. It is a simple enough task, if we stick to the model, but it is seldom an easy one.

Most organizations and the business community as a whole are currently to be found in the *assertion* stage, but they are increasingly aspiring to *cooperation*. This shift from *assertion* to *cooperation* encapsulates the nature of the culture change which the next chapter addresses.

7
Business Culture Change

Let's now look more specifically at the process of culture change or continuous transformation in business. These terms are all too frequently just words which roll easily off the tongue at business gatherings. Nevertheless, the notion that business has to change its culture is becoming widely accepted. Even though the phrase 'if it is to survive' has recently been added without much dissent, few business people comprehend the degree of change and commitment that will be called for in the years to come.

Internal culture

A change of culture, yes, but what from and what to? The answers one receives to these questions depend more on perspective than on consensus, but in terms of our three-stage model it is the shift from *assertion* to *cooperation*. When this shift occurs in teams, collective performance rises, and most business people would agree that any change in the business culture has to be driven by higher levels of performance. How can this be achieved at a time when opportunities for promotion and pay increases are shrinking in most sectors?

Coaching and teamwork
Whereas a few years ago our clients would approach us to run a coaching skills workshop for a dozen of their best, or sometimes their worst, managers, now they are more often wanting to change the culture of the organization. However, a series of culture change workshops might sound too fuzzy to some and too threatening to others, but 'coaching' and 'teambuilding' are readily acceptable, and

these skills are the building blocks of both cultural change and performance improvement.

My colleagues and I specialize in coaching and teambuilding, because these are our fields of particular expertise, but more importantly because these are the practical skills of the new era of *cooperation* into which business has to evolve. Besides, culture change needs to be driven by clear corporate performance objectives and in response to the changing conditions of the corporate environment. A change of culture because that is what others are doing or because it seems a good idea may be commendable, but will almost certainly result in a poorly integrated change programme.

New game, old rules

Many organizations have already reached the peak of their *assertion* stage and it is time to begin the transformation into *cooperation*. However, business leaders who have climbed to the top of the *assertion* ladder face a paradox. They won the game under the old rules and now expect to, and are expected to, lead the way in a very different game. Many of them know about the new game. They are highly intelligent, well read and well informed about trends. Intellectually they advocate and are aware of the performance benefits of coaching and the qualities and principles of *cooperation*. They recommend them to others, even demand them of their staff. They send their staff on teambuilding programmes, outward bound, survival courses, you name it.

Their own behaviour, however, often remains totally unchanged, although they themselves believe that their actions reflect their words. Their staff, disappointed to experience little change at the top, become disillusioned and their hope and enthusiasm for change within the organization die.

In my experience real organizational transformation only occurs when the chief executive and the board actively engage alongside their staff in their own training, and then truly walk their talk.

The changed company

So what would a change from *assertion* values to *cooperation* values mean in practical terms? For many organizations it would mean a flatter hierarchy, self-directed teams, devolved responsibility, less formality, honest and open feedback in all directions, a no-blame culture, refocusing on quality, genuine customer care, environmental and ethical responsibility, flexible working practices, greater choice and ownership at every level, a coaching management style, shared goals, a learning organization and of course the overused and under-understood term, empowerment.

Nothing new there – but achieving that much will take most companies long enough, and there will still be plenty more changes to come. I say nothing new, because these concepts are talked about and written about *ad nauseam* in business circles, but hardly ever put into practice. There are, however, some examples of good practice. The most applauded is Semco in Brazil, and another, a Wisconsin-based food company, which goes by the unlikely name of Johnsonville Sausage! These two *cooperative* companies and a few others like them still manage to be highly successful even by the conventional criteria of business today which remains predominantly *assertive*.

Semco

Semco's president, Ricardo Semler, is now a highly sought-after speaker at business seminars and has been voted Latin American Businessman of the Year. His revolutionary article 'Managing without Managers' in the *Harvard Business Review* and his book *Maverick* tell the story of his company's transformation over a period of ten years from a highly *assertive*, hierarchical organization to a model of *cooperation*.

The dust jacket of *Maverick* summarizes Semco's transformation as follows:

> Since he succeeded his father as head of the family firm Semco, a manufacturer of pumps, mixers, valves and other industrial equipment, Semler has spent his time dismantling the corporate hierarchy and turning the traditional idea of a business organization on its head. He began by throwing out all the company rules – today Semco has almost no manuals or written procedures – and he insisted that the workers made the decisions previously made by the boss. All employees are treated as responsible adults, and most set their own working hours. They all have access to the

> company books and vote on important company decisions. Most of the managerial staff set their own salaries and bonuses. This unorthodox approach has been vastly successful.

Johnsonville Sausage

Ralph Stayer is the chief executive of Johnsonville Sausage, though he now prefers to see himself as a consultant to the company. He stated in 1990: 'When I began this process of change ten years ago, I looked forward to the time when it would be all over and I could get back to my real job. But I've learned that change is the real job of every effective business leader because change is about the present and the future not about the past.'

Much is made today of the value of being a learning organization, but, like mission and value statements, the words alone are meaningless. Ralph Stayer again:

> The end state we all now envision for Johnsonville is a company that never stops learning. . . the most important kind of learning teaches us to question our own actions and behaviour in order to better understand the ways we perform, work and live. Helping human beings fulfil their potential is of course a moral responsibility, but it is also good for business. Life is aspiration. Learning, striving people are happy people and good workers. They have initiative and imagination, and the companies they work for are rarely caught napping.

What these two business leaders possess, what is required and all too often sadly lacking are vision, courage, commitment and a role model at the top. It can be done: they have done it and succeeded in a period of great economic uncertainty. They have played the *cooperation* game when the world around them was playing the *assertion* game, and they ended up winning both. It may soon become less risky to embark on a process of fundamental culture change than to remain static and be washed up by the tide of change.

'To survive in modern times,' Ricardo Semler writes in *Maverick*, 'a company must have an organizational structure that accepts change as its basic premise, lets tribal customs thrive, and fosters a power that is derived from respect, not rules. In other words, the successful companies will be the ones that put quality of life first. Do this and the rest – quality of product, productivity of workers, profits for all – will follow.'

Simple as that may sound, the risks of initiating major corporate changes are great; however, the risks of continuing to juggle with people, products, processes and profits for short-term gain or survival may turn out to be even greater. No one will claim that it is easy to create the successful organization of the future by recycling a dinosaur without killing it at the same time. Semler again:

> At Semco we did away with strictures that dictate the 'hows' and created fertile soil for differences. We gave people an opportunity to test, question and disagree. We let them determine their own training and their own futures. We let them come and go as they wanted, work at home if they wished, set their own salaries, choose their own bosses. We let them change their minds and ours, prove us wrong when we are wrong, make us humbler. Such a system relishes change, which is the only antidote to the corporate brainwashing that has consigned giant businesses with brilliant pasts to uncertain futures.

Blame in business

Into an earlier list of characteristics of a changed company I slipped a 'no-blame culture', which is probably the least easy concept for many managers to accept. Blame is endemic in business; managers are expected to blame. However, blame works against good performance for the following reasons:

❏ Blame focuses attention away from the task on to fear and punishment.
❏ Blame evokes justifications and excuses, not the truth.
❏ Only where there is truth can there be proper evaluation.
❏ Only where there is proper evaluation can there be correction.
❏ Blame reduces risk taking, innovation and creativity.

❏ Blame reduces self-esteem, confidence and learning from mistakes.
❏ Blame undermines trust, support, communication and honesty.

Honesty, openness and trust

Many managers live under the illusion that they can lie to their staff or withhold the obvious from them. They treat their staff like children, but neither staff nor children are fools. Managers frequently end up discrediting themselves. This is what Semler has to say about it: 'Workers are adults, but once they walk through the plant gate companies transform them into children, forcing them to wear identification badges, stand in line for lunch, ask the foreman for permission to go to the bathroom, bring in a doctor's note when they have been ill and blindly follow instructions without asking any questions.'

Worker searches had been a part of life at Semco, but Semler eliminated them, saying, 'I wasn't under the illusion that, by eliminating searches, we would eliminate thefts. I'll bet that on average two or three percent of any work force will take advantage of an employer's trust. But is this a valid reason to subject 97 percent to a daily ritual of humiliation? Yes, there will be theft here and embezzlement there, but that's the case in companies with huge auditing and monitoring departments. It's a cost of doing business. I would rather have a few thefts once in a while than condemn everyone to a system based on mistrust.' Perhaps when the most senior people in the business community begin to show a little more honesty, integrity and ethics than some of them do at present, the concern about trust at other levels will be restored; I will return to that issue in a later chapter. A final word from Ricardo Semler:

The sad truth is that employees of modern corporations have little reason to feel satisfied, much less fulfilled. Companies do not have the time or the interest to listen to them, and lack the resources or the inclination to train for advancement. These companies make a series of demands, for which they compensate employees with salaries that are often considered inadequate. Moreover, companies tend to be implacable in dismissing workers when they start to age or go through a temporary drop in performance, and send people into retirement earlier than they want, leaving the feeling that they could have contributed much more had someone just asked.

The era of using people as production tools is coming to an end. Participation is infinitely more complex to practise than conventional corporate unilateralism, just as democracy is much more cumbersome than dictatorship. But there will be few companies that can afford to ignore either of them.

Integrated culture

So far we have looked at some of the elements of culture change in so far as they affect the internal workings of an organization. For many years the focus of businesses has been on themselves, what they do, how they do it, how they present themselves, how well organized they are and how profitable they are. 'Punters' and even small shareholders were seen as a necessary evil or an interference in the daily routine. Britain was a relatively late starter in the rather obvious need to question this introspective focus, and to shift it to the people who should matter most, the customers.

Customer care

In recent years customer care initiatives have been taken by nearly every business organization. Instead of making what they want to make and telling the customer that they need it and can't have anything else, businesses have begun to ask what the customer wants and then try to supply it. As with all forms of change, it tends to begin with the words rather than the actions, so we see lots of 'We take care of our customers' proclamations while nothing has really changed. Some customers are gullible enough to believe the hype over their own experience, but the vast majority become disillusioned when they find business as usual. The next step, which most companies are yet to take, is to care for the customer instead of just talking about it.

Here is an anecdote that illustrates blame, lack of responsibility, poor role models, lip service rather than authenticity, poor staff relations and words, not deeds. What happened was done with the best intentions but with little vision and understanding. I have changed some aspects of the story to disguise the company involved.

> The top management of a chain with outlets on every high street rightly deemed it desirable to improve customer relations. They commissioned a survey among customers to ascertain what behaviours from the sales and service staff would make the customer feel cared for. They informed the staff of their findings and after a while arranged for some mystery shoppers to pose as customers and then rate the performance of staff against this list of criteria. In a short time the rating improved dramatically, but the company also had the wisdom to conduct interviews with customers to see if they felt better cared for. Surprisingly, the results this time showed that things were getting worse.
>
> What had happened was that the staff had learned the criteria by rote and were using them regularly but inauthentically. Therefore their ratings went up, but their lack of authenticity made the customer feel less cared for: the 'Have a nice day' syndrome.

Customer care cannot be fudged. If customers are cared for, they will *feel* cared for. If they are not, no amount of clever phrases will suffice. You can tell the quality of the management of a restaurant by the way the waiters and waitresses treat the diners: one is a reflection of the other. Staff relations were poor right through the company discussed above, and this was reflected at the point of contact with the customer in the high street. The problem was born in the boardroom, but instead of the top management taking responsibility for it, they shifted the blame to the most junior level in the organization in the hope that it would go away. It won't. Only when each level in the organization cares for the next level down, only when it reaches the customer, will customer care be really taken care of. There are no short cuts, and the price of doing nothing is high.

New values

As organizations, led with vision or driven by necessity, move cautiously into the culture of *cooperation*, at first internally and later externally with their customers, the local community and eventually with their erstwhile competitors, they will increasingly embrace and express new values. Openness and honesty are essential in a *cooperative* culture, therefore those dubious things that the corporation was secretive about have to be abandoned or cleaned up. Sharp practices, slush funds, sleaze, cartels, price fixing, insider trading, backhanders and golden handshakes have no place to hide in an open and honest, *cooperative* corporation.

Behavioural change may come first, but they must soon be followed by a real change in attitude and values. As we move towards a more *cooperative* society, not only will companies be run on more internally *cooperative* management principles, but they will find themselves beginning to *cooperate* with the wider community. At the same time the nature of the products and services that they offer will begin to change from seductive but useless or obsolescent consumer products, which feed our egos and our **greed** rather than our **need**, towards those that are more socially useful and healthy.

New products

In fact this is already beginning to happen. Major supermarkets are stocking more and more organically grown produce, Swatches are replacing Rolexes, fur coats are out and recycling is in. Most components of today's new cars are recyclable. All major motor manufacturers have alternative and low-energy vehicle research projects, and I look forward to the arrival of the modern equivalent of the Ford Popular or the Model-T. The growth of charity shops and car boot sales also reflects more *cooperative* social values. These changes seem to arise randomly and some of them fail, but looked at as a whole they signify the first tentative steps of the evolutionary march of our collective social culture towards *cooperation*. Maslow's higher needs are just beginning to be addressed.

Wider responsibility

It may be hard to imagine *cooperative* qualities ever becoming the new criteria by which businesses of the future are measured, and by which the business community at large operates. Is it too far-fetched then to imagine the businesses and industries of a whole country *cooperating* with one another, and placing the good of the community or the country above the profits of each separately owned business? How about the global business community *cooperating* for the good of the whole of society, all five and a half billion members of it?

8
Business Ethics

Many companies publish mission statements, often accompanied and supported by a set of values to which the company and staff are supposed to aspire. In the main these concern the internal workings of the company and its relationship to its customers. They can be seen to be a precursor to the *cooperation* stage – *cooperation* among those immediately affected by the business. As with most gradual change processes, the concept and the words precede the behaviour and herald its manifestation. They are a sign of hope, a sign that the *co-operation* stage may be not too far over the horizon.

Mission statements

Mission statements began to be adopted by organizations in the 1980s to provide a focal point and to establish the corporate values. Most companies found it much easier to string the words together than to live up to their meaning. This in turn resulted in a growing cynicism about mission statements. Here are some examples:

- ❑ To become one of the best financial services groups in the eyes of our customers, staff and shareholders.
- ❑ To provide a wide range of safe and rewarding personal financial services based on its core business of residential mortgage lending.
- ❑ Famous for delighting customers with high performance service and products.
- ❑ Our mission is to flourish as a leading provider of quality financial products, offering customers the best possible service and above average performance, backed by high standards of ethics and integrity.

Values

In addition, many companies put together a comprehensive set of values which they display and circulate to their staff and sometimes their customers. These are often subject to the same fate as mission statements because there is seldom any concerted effort to ensure that they are adopted. The 'how to' is easily missed, and in any case just telling people 'how to' is seldom enough. Values that are expressed as attitudes have to be converted into practical behaviours, but behaviours acted out without the genuine underlying attitude to go with them produce phoniness. It is possible for a company, a chief executive or a manager to demand certain behaviours, but a good attitude is not a demandable commodity. It is achieved only by having good role models and a supportive or coaching management style. This calls for genuine commitment from the very top, not just fine words.

General Accident Insurance, based in York, England, has the following values statement:

We value:
'Can do' people who show Initiative and Determination
Relationships that are based on Fairness, Care and Respect
Nimble teams that achieve through Individual Accountability
Thinking that is Broad, Creative and Flexible
Communication that is Direct and Readily Understood

This is an admirable set of values, which emphasize people and which is entirely in line both with the principles of a coaching management style and with the *cooperation* stage. Below is another set of values from a building society espousing similar behavioural qualities, but they are somewhat more business oriented:

1 Keep our name synonymous with quality and value in customer service.
2 Aim to keep our customers for life.
3 Always be open and honest.
4 Run the business effectively and profitably.

5 Build team spirit.
6 Provide appropriate support and authority to staff.
7 Be bold in the exercise of authority.
8 Make decision-making as streamlined as possible.
9 Make jobs stimulating and enjoyable.
10 Train well to fulfil our responsibilities.

The following more extensive and very commendable list is from a main high street bank, though I was disappointed to find how few of its staff had come across it:

1 **We approach every aspect of our work with the highest standards of integrity.**
❏ We act with the highest levels of honesty and integrity in all that we do.
❏ We take full responsibility for our decisions and actions.
❏ We admit to our mistakes, so that the effect on customers or colleagues can be put right quickly.
❏ We make a positive contribution to the social and economic well-being of the communities in which we operate.

2 **We value our customers.**
❏ We aim to be the first choice for our customers.
❏ We make our customers' problems our own – and we resolve them.
❏ If customers complain, our aim is to send them away satisfied and pleased with our response.

3 **We approach our work as a professional team.**
❏ We constantly look for ways to improve the quality of what we produce, whether as individuals or teams.
❏ We work until the result is achieved, not just the specific tasks that are given to us.
❏ We operate in teams, within and across business lines, wherever this will improve the quality of work and services we deliver.

4 We treat each other as we wish to be treated ourselves.

❏ We share the successes, problems and disappointments of colleagues across the group and we frown on those who denigrate others' efforts.

❏ If we are disappointed with the contribution of colleagues, we discuss with them how it can be improved – we don't complain behind their backs.

❏ We help colleagues to fulfil family and other responsibilities outside work.

❏ We set a personal example to all colleagues in observing these values, particularly those who look to us for leadership, guidance or help.

Some more forward-thinking companies are beginning to consider *cooperation* beyond the confines of the business and its customers, with society as a whole. This means not only looking at how the company relates to the immediate community in which it is located, but at how it affects the local and wider environment, and the degree to which its products and services benefit or debase society in general. This is a much more controversial area because it introduces ethics and moral judgement.

Personal ethics

No two people will agree on what is ethically correct, especially in business where there are often a number of conflicting interests. The law is a very specific set of rules about what is acceptable and what is not, but even laws often have to be tested in the courts for interpretation. The law was supposed to be about justice, but in recent years Britain has been drifting the way of the United States. There the law and justice parted company a long time ago, and it is all down to what you can legally get away with. Morals are often considered to be prescribed by religion or bodies which create other codes that call on us to behave in a certain manner.

Ethics are much more down to the individual and his or her own conscience, so standards vary quite widely. Ethical positions are based

on many considerations: qualitative, humanitarian, personal upbringing, health and the feel good factor. It is clear that it is ethically
more sound to do something for the good of the whole than just for
the good of oneself. What we determine to constitute the whole will
be governed by the limit of our own ego boundaries. For some the
whole may mean their team, but for others it is their region, for some
it is the company, for others it is the nation and for yet others the only
whole is all of humanity (*see* the discussion of ego boundaries in
chapter 11).

People will vigorously defend the validity of their particular limits,
but the only truly *cooperative* boundary will contain all of humanity.
On that basis, ethics may well demand that employees have a higher
order of allegiance to humanity than to their company. This may
result in conflict, which could lead to disaffected staff and a whistle
blower or two. As people and society at large grow, evolve and
mature, their ethical standards rise. If directors and senior managers
do not recognize this and raise their own standards at at least the
same rate, they risk criticism from their own staff and from outside.
I say directors and senior managers here, rather than company,
because there is no such thing as an ethical organization: only people
can be ethical.

In the UK and USA in recent years there have been a spate of inci-
dents where corporations and senior executives have been brought to
book for unacceptable behaviour. This is behaviour that may or may
not have been entirely legal, but was accepted practice in the past.
When they were exposed, some of them felt unfairly persecuted or
prosecuted for doing what they had always done. They had failed to
keep pace with the evolving attitudes of society.

Nothing undermines the credibility of big business and top
management more in the eyes of both their own staff and the general public than the perception that they are **greedy**. If their rewards are
excessive or increase at a rate above that of staff or at a time of staff
redundancies which have been explained by a need to tighten the corporate belt, people will be disgusted. In 1995 Cedric Brown, the then
chief executive of British Gas, took a pay rise of 75 per cent up to
£475,000 per annum at the very time that his company was laying off
8,000 staff and customer complaints were soaring. This triggered the

Cartoon copyright 1995 by Herblock in *The Washington Post*.

public uproar which resulted in the Greenbury Report on executive pay. The Conservative government, as the British public had grown to expect, failed to condemn this **greed**, shuffled uncomfortably, made a few U-turns and also lost public respect. What is so surprising is not that Brown, and others like him, attempt unconvincingly to justify their pay, but that they are so unaware of the potential for public condemnation. Either that or they simply don't care, and their personal **greed** overrides all other considerations. There will be no place whatsoever for Cedric Brown (who retired 'hurt' in April 1996) and his ilk in the corporate cultures of the future.

An organization is going to have to adopt the highest possible standards if it is to retain the respect and support of its staff, its customers and its public reputation. What this means is: 'If in doubt, do the right thing.' On the other hand, it would be a mistake to get too far ahead of public attitudes and start moralizing. We cannot lecture people about what ethical standards they should adopt, but we can communicate clearly what our own ethical standards are. If we communicate them, we have to live up to them or we become highly vulnerable to criticism. In 1994 Anita Roddick and The Body Shop became exposed and chastened by revelations that they were not as environmentally friendly as they claimed to be, although most of these were unfounded, and they are now proselytizing in a lower key as a result, probably to better effect.

The emerging ethical values in society and in business are already affecting a wide range of aspects of business relating to both people and products:

❑ The way staff are treated, management style, redundancies, pensions etc.
❑ The way the environment is treated, including waste, recycling.
❑ The way suppliers are treated, particularly suppliers in developing countries.
❑ Fair remuneration for all, with an eye on executive excesses.
❑ Concerns about aggressive selling and misleading advertising.
❑ Internal and external openness and honesty.
❑ Health and welfare considerations for staff including stress, the demands of parenting etc.
❑ Sexual equality, positive racial attitudes and avoidance of harrassment.
❑ Executives expected to be role models and set examples.
❑ Products that offer genuine value.
❑ Products that are socially beneficial, or at least neutral.
❑ Products that put people (humanity) before profit; which confronts tobacco companies and the arms trade, for example.
❑ Concerns over the use of hazardous or environmentally dangerous chemicals.
❑ How the company relates to the community, charities etc.

Any company which disregards any of these areas is at risk of criticism from without and within. And what is acceptable today may no longer be acceptable tomorrow. Any company with vision, however, will not just be keeping pace with the public mood, but will want to be ahead of the game, for several reasons:

❑ They will want to be seen to be a leading company.

❑ The executive and senior management need to be role models for their staff, and earn their respect.

❑ The most alert of their staff will be ahead of the rest anyway and they risk alienating their best people.

❑ The risk of a boycott of goods and services increases as the public becomes more aware, and aware of its power.

❑ There is a time lag, particularly in a large organization, between the words and the collective adoption of suitable behaviours.

❑ Standards do not remain static but continue to rise as society evolves.

By far the most important is that they have a responsibility to society.

'That is not our business', they may say. Well, whose business is it then? The governments'? But who holds the economic power? Who is responsible for being responsible? We all are. But if businesses are concerned about their own long-term sustainability and survival, they may have to become globally responsible.

Responsibility to society

People look to governments for leadership, to lead the country to the promised land – but they will be disappointed. Most politicians any-where these days are too busy playing politics to govern with wisdom or vision. Decisions are made and half-truths are told for short-term political expediency on political grounds rather than according to real national or global needs. Unfortunately that is the way it is likely to continue in the immediate future. For a variety of reasons politi-cians are not providing the kind of leadership that our world needs. At the same time, multinational corporations are wielding more and more economic and social power, aided by the communication revo-lution. The economy of many large corporations exceeds that of many countries. Countries are getting smaller and more prolific while corporations are merging to get even bigger.

Who is it then that controls the economy? Surely it is big business rather than politics. The trouble is that there is a fundamental flaw in the global economy, which is so blindingly obvious that few of us seem to see it. The economy has lost its rightful purpose.

People are now in service to the economy, instead of the economy being in service to people.

People are sacrificed daily for the sake of the economy:

❏ We make people redundant with little thought for the social consequences.

❏ We cannot put in disabled facilities because it is not commercially viable.

❏ We cannot agree to the European Social Chapter because our economy will suffer.

❏ We cannot make our ferries safe because it is too expensive.

❏ We cannot afford these drugs, this operation or to keep this hospital open.

The list of examples could be endless, and of course we have to draw the line somewhere and create a balance. It is just that the line at present is on the side of the economy, not on the side of people. Until and unless we put people first (*cooperation*), economies and currencies will increasingly be manipulated and destabilized by the **greed** (*assertion*) of money market Mafia.

It would make social sense to redefine the economy, and then redesign it as 'An efficient and effective means of enabling 5.5 billion people on planet earth to exchange goods and services to meet their **needs**'. The phrase 'but not their **greeds**', might be added to make the purpose absolutely clear. But at present that would not be an attractive proposition to those interested in political power or commercial growth. I am treading on dangerous ground here since this sounds a bit like communism – or *cooperation* or Christian values – but then Jesus has often been accused of being a communist!

Such an economy would be ideal if we, the people of the world, had reached the *cooperation* stage in our evolution. However we, or at least the rich and powerful people and nations, are firmly installed in the *assertion* stage, and we have an economy to suit that – to suit our **greeds**. We design our social systems to suit our present level of maturity, and then the system takes over and keeps us at that level. It requires courage and persistence to run our lives or our organizations along *cooperative* lines, within an economic system designed for *assertion*.

So the structure of our economy makes it easier for us to keep playing the *assertion* game, just as the structure of our companies encourages directors and senior management to maintain *assertive* behaviour. All the mission statements and values are meaningless in an organizational structure that does not support them. Some businesses are flattening their hierarchy, sometimes out of necessity rather than choice, but it is a start. Some are devolving power to self-directed teams, which is progress; but how many businesses are changing the power structure at the top? Semco and Johnsonville Sausage are two and of course there are many more, but not nearly enough.

How many large corporations have contribution to society as their principal goal?

Two industries which confront our ethics – or should do – are the tobacco industry and the arms trade. They are large, powerful, assertive and pervasive, and they directly or indirectly negatively influence each of us and our collective culture. They are driven, more than most industries, by **greed**. They are the antithesis of the values and practice of *cooperation*.

It must be remembered that these industries were established long before the dangers of smoking were recognized and when arms were legitimately needed for national defence. Then they were considered as legitimate and respectable as any other business. However, any pre-existing justification falls apart once smoking is known to kill in vast numbers and when weapons are being sold for profit with little discrimination. Of course, both industries provide employment for a considerable number of people, but the provision of jobs alone can never be claimed to be a valid reason for a harmful business activity. There are, after all, plenty of valuable life-giving jobs which need to be done, and not enough people doing them.

The tobacco industry

The annual world-wide sales of the tobacco industry amount to $200 billion. European governments provide a vast tobacco subsidy to growers in the European Union, mainly in Turkey, amounting to over

In 1992 Margaret Thatcher accepted a contract with tobacco company Philip Morris to advise on its strategy in the developing world.

£800 million per annum, more than that given for any other crop through the Common Agricultural policy. Britain alone contributes £50 million of this, which is equal to the amount the whole of Europe spends on its anti-cancer campaign. The fact that health ministers struggle to restrict smoking while chancellors happily benefit from it is further evidence of the schizophrenia of politicians. In the United States alone over 350,000 people die every year from smoking-related diseases, and smoking has been identified by the government as the primary preventable cause of death.

It is almost beyond my comprehension that human beings can justify to themselves actively working for a business whose prime product is known to cause untold health problems and death, with all the attendant suffering, for no tangible benefit whatsoever.

'It's a job,' they will say, perhaps the only job available. That may be true for the plantation workers, but it becomes less and less true as we go up the corporate ladder to heights at which we would hope to find higher levels of social responsibility. What we find instead is **greed**, and to hell with the consequences.

'No one is forced to smoke,' they will say. No, but nicotine is one of the most addictive substances around and the power of advertising overwhelms the vulnerable.

'If I did not do this job someone else would,' they will say. True, but does that justify them personally being engaged in killing people?

'Everyone has a right to smoke, it is a civil liberty. If they choose to kill themselves it's their business,' they will say. That is a high-minded ideal, but it is not true. My right to clean air is a prior right. And if smokers use up a large proportion of a limited health budget, which they do, then I am also affected.

'Advertising does not cause people to smoke, only to switch brands,' they will say, but this is untrue and they know it. Documentation has been leaked which clearly indicates that some tobacco advertising has been targeted at under-age people. This is a well-known technique of starting people on the right brand, leading to brand loyalty.

'The link between cigarettes and heart disease and lung cancer has never been absolutely established. There was a study which…' There will always be unscrupulous doctors and scientists who can be bought. Any honest person can hardly fail to be aware of the overwhelming evidence of the health hazards of smoking which have emerged from hundreds of studies.

Larry White has written an excellent and very persuasive book about the unethical nature of the tobacco industry, *The Merchants of Death*, which I would recommend.

The arms trade

There is a sort of shady underworld comprised of arms dealers, people with connections to the CIA, certain retired military men, respectable looking right-wing politicians, Swiss bankers and dictators from countries that would be developing if the dictator was not spending the budget on arms to keep the army on his side. There is a strange similarity in the relationship between Conservative politicians and the arms business in Britain, and that between the Republican party and the National Rifle Association in the United States. I would not dare to suggest any conspiratorial link: the link is a psychological one. How many more psychological steps down the same path do we have to take before we meet the pathological mass killer in battle fatigues shooting up Hungerford or a school in Dunblane or blowing up Oklahoma City or Centennial Park. Isn't weaponry the ultimate tool of *assertion* for psychologically inadequate people with big fears or big egos?

We have all heard the old canards about the need to defend ourselves and our allies against an aggressor, and the deterrent effect of having an army which is well trained and equipped. We have heard how important the arms trade is to our aircraft industry, the balance of payments and the employment figures. We have heard that soldiers fight wars and that civilians are protected by the Geneva Convention or will be by the United Nations. We know that the development costs of our defence weapons have to be amortized over larger numbers of weapons sold to third parties. We know that there are government regulations to prevent the arms we sell from falling into the wrong hands. There is more than a grain of truth in all these arguments and there are no simple answers. The problem is we also know that governments lie, that civilians aren't always protected, that weapons fall into the hands of anyone who wants them enough, and that some people make an awful lot of money out of the arms trade.

There is no prescription for the abolition or abandonment of weapons. Even in 1996 the UN could not agree to impose an absolute ban on landmines, which account for thousands of killings and maimings of civilians in many countries every year long after the hostilities are over. However, we all possess the power of personal choice. What follows is not an exhaustive, balanced or unbiased set of statistics. They are not intended to prove anything, but to provoke thought:

1   Britain is one of the world's leading arms exporters, along with the USA, Russia, Germany, France and China.
2   Over £1,900 million worth of military equipment left the UK for overseas countries in 1993.
3   In 1993 Britain accepted new orders for arms totalling £6,000 million.

4   Nearly two-thirds of British arms exports in 1993 went to Third World countries.

5   Britain has been a major and consistent arms supplier to Indonesia, which illegally invaded East Timor in 1975 and continues viciously to suppress the population there.

6   For the price of one British Aerospace Hawk aircraft, 1.5 million people in the Third World could have clean water for life.

7   One-fifth of the current Third World debt is down to money loaned for arms purchases in the 1970s.

8   The £234 million of British aid granted to Malaysia for the highly contentious Pergau Dam project was directly linked to a £1 billion arms deal.

9   British jobs directly or indirectly depend on arms exports.

10   Overall arms sales to Third World countries in 1993 amounted to more than $25 billion.

11   In 1994 the United States and Russia possessed 16,900 strategic and 27,000 non-strategic nuclear warheads between them.

12   Britain has between 250 and 300 operational nuclear warheads today. This alone is sufficient effectively to wipe out life on earth.

13   Hungary, Poland and the Czech Republic have recently been seeking to buy 200 advanced jet fighters for some $8 billion.

14   In July 1996 a British trial jury acquitted four female peace campaigners who broke into a British Aerospace factory and caused damage amounting to £1.5 million to a Hawk military plane destined for Indonesia. It considered their actions 'lawful' – so do I.

We can make responsible decisions to renounce weapons and denounce the arms business. We can refuse to deal with any firm engaged in the arms business. We can each make our own effort and contribution to moving ourselves and those whom we touch towards, or further into, the *cooperation* stage, where there is no place for the arms trade and ultimately no need for weapons. Nothing will happen overnight except we may sleep more soundly and be able to look at ourselves more comfortably in the morning mirror.

Grey areas

There are other industries – for example gambling, pharmaceuticals, agrochemicals, producers of substitute baby milk, junk food and confectionery, pornography and video games – which may not be so black, but which may be tinged with various shades of grey depending on your ethical stance.

This grey area will be by far the largest category for most people, which is precisely why it is so important for each of us to be aware of what we are making, buying and using, and the choices we make on a daily basis. The Consumers' Association magazine, *Which?*, and another called *The Ethical Consumer* may help us make those choices; although if you read the latter thoroughly you may begin to wonder what you *can* consume ethically.

Where do we start?

If we believe we must change the culture of our business or of the world economy, where do we start? With the people or with the system? The answer must be both, and if one or other gets too far ahead, there will be a breakdown. Imposing democracy or demanding cooperation are unacceptable contradictions. Both Semler and Stayer found that bringing about the changes they envisioned required sensitive handling, even though they were clearly beneficial to everyone. Here are a few guidelines:

❑ If we radically and too quickly redesign our company structure, we are liable to get too far ahead of our staff. A valid caution, but most of us will be far too slow to change!

❑ If we impose our redesign on our staff, they are liable to object even if it is intended to be entirely for their benefit.

❑ We must first help the staff to develop themselves and experiment with some of the attitudes and behaviours that one would expect in a *cooperative* organization.

❑ The executive and senior management must, from the very beginning, set the example, and model the ideal attitudes and behaviours authentically and well.

❑ Staff cannot be forced to change, but need the opportunity to choose how to change.

❑ Without a collective vision change cannot succeed, but without vision at the top it will not even start.

❑ It is hard for an *assertive* autocrat to make a decent job of change.

Business leaders and businesses have a huge responsibility to lead the way out of the social inequity created globally by our inept and inefficient economic system. They may not want that task or that responsibility – but if they don't take it on, who is going to? Who else has the power and the knowledge? Politicians do not. And business has vast human resources of the very best talent for leadership. That talent at present is in the main directed towards *assertive* means to *assertive* ends, but it could and should be increasingly redirecting itself towards *cooperation*. This is not such a big shift for them, because a few chief executives of multinational corporations are now at least talking about major internal change, the values of which are those of *cooperation*. It can't be too difficult for them to raise their eyes to see a wider vision for society, or to raise their sights to achieving it.

Their initial *assertive* thought may be 'What is in it for us?', but they have already been asking themselves that question about their internal culture change, and found the right answer – survival. If that was true about their company, why should it not also be true of society? A better reason to *cooperate* is because it will help to make a better world. This may not be an overly compelling motivation for some business people, consumed by firefighting or the profit motive, but it will become ever more so.

Another attractive reason for business leaders to take more responsibility for the world is that then they can make it the way they want it. We left it to politicians, and look at the mess they made of it! As they become less and less relevant, who is going to fill the vacuum? If business people, who have the power, don't take the responsibility, an organization such as Greenpeace just might show the way. It has a global vision, it is into *cooperation*, it captured the Brent Spar and the public imagination, and it is very clear about some of the things we need to change if this planet is to survive. The business community would be wise to consider the consequences of not taking more global responsibility, if they wish to remain in control of their own destiny.

Corporate leaders have a unique opportunity, now more than ever, to make the world just the way they want it, but it remains to be seen if old behaviours of *assertion* erupt again or if new principles of *co-operation* manage to prevail. At a gathering of 200 top executives held at the Royal Society of Arts in London in June 1995, a research document entitled *Tomorrow's Company: The Role of Business in a Changing World* was released. The research reinforces the need for what I describe as the move towards *cooperative* values and suggests that in future companies will increasingly be beholden to their stakeholders rather than their shareholders. The stakeholders would include the employees, the customers, the local community, the environment, the general public and of course the shareholders, but the latter would be unlikely to head the list. British Labour leader Tony Blair was quick to adopt the stakeholder slogan. The shareholder of a future business less driven by profit might fit more into the category of custodian than that of gambler.

This is a fundamental shift, but it is in the air. People's personal attitudes are changing too. More and more people are looking to their job not only for income, security and satisfaction, but also to be making a social contribution, or at least to be neutral in terms of its social impact. Maslow's higher needs are to the fore once more.

Cooperation may eventually be essential for humankind's collective survival. Fortunately, human evolution is on the side of the collective good, and it occurs in spite of us. We can slow it down a little, as we have, or we can accelerate it, as we have to. The choice is ours.

9
Economics and the Environment

Humanity pays a huge premium for continuing to indulge itself in the *assertion* stage. In this chapter we examine the cost of non-*cooperation* to ourselves, our children and ultimately to the economy. I have claimed that people are in service to the economy rather than the economy being in service to people. However, it is not only people who are subjugated and subordinated to the economy, it is our whole planet. The economy as it is structured today for growth and **greed** in the short term is destroying lives, our livelihood and threatens to destroy life itself. If that seems exaggerated or overstated, it is because most people, most business people in particular, choose to close their eyes to the environmental impact of their actions.

When environmentalism first appeared on the corporate agenda, it was little more than an act of tokenism in an attempt to defuse and disarm what were perceived as irritating and fanatical do-gooders. Much PR was made out of the formation of an environmental department, the employment of an environmental officer, green rural settings for advertisements for noxious products, a small donation to 'Save the Seagulls' or the undertaking of a minuscule environmental research project. It was an improvement in behaviour perhaps, or at least it gave the outward appearance of it.

At the same time individuals began to recycle their cans, glass and newspapers, to consume less energy for economical but also for ecological reasons, to switch to diesel or unleaded petrol, to specify recycled paper and to seek out organically grown produce. Unfortunately these small actions, commendable as they are, lull us into the illusion that we are solving the environmental problem. I claim emphatically that:

❏ we have not scratched the surface of the problem;
❏ we are ignorant of and blind to the problem;
❏ a complete reordering of business, economics and our thinking is required;
❏ we owe nothing less to our children.

With the passage of time and the push of some governmental legislation, the more visible heavy industrial polluters have been obliged to begin to change their ways, albeit reluctantly. Greenpeace and animal rights protesters have helped us become more aware of some of the more harmful excesses of business – or have driven us to pompous reactionary responses. They both have used media spectaculars for their purposes, because they know that 'conventional channels' are ineffective and that public awareness and bad publicity will move business – eventually.

Public opinion

Shell's *débâcle* over the planned sinking of the Brent Spar platform was a classic case of business massively underestimating the growing public social and environmental concern. Regardless of the contaminants the platform contained, or the pros and cons of deep-sea disposal in that particular case, this example was perhaps the first great victory of social concern over a perceived bad business choice. Within months Shell was on the ropes again, unsuccessfully defending itself for the environmental damage caused by its oil extraction in Southern Nigeria, the home of the Ogoni ethnic group, and for failing to prevent the execution in November 1995 of Ken Saro-Wiwa, the leader of the Ogoni people's protest, and eight 'co-conspirators' by the corrupt Nigerian military rulers. Since oil accounts for 90 per cent of Nigeria's export income and Shell was the principal player, and since Shell was on the verge of signing a £2.6 billion gas contract with the country, it could have exerted huge pressure on the military junta to spare Saro-Wiwa.

It is unlikely that Shell will be so cavalier about ethical choices and public opinion in future, and other companies will no doubt take note. Neither the action of Greenpeace nor the world-wide condemnation of France's decision to conduct a series of nuclear test explosions in the South Pacific moved the determined President Chirac. Even he, however, must have been surprised by the boycotting of French goods thereafter by many ordinary people around the world. British Prime Minister John Major, with characteristic ineptitude and environmental callousness, was the only leader at the Commonwealth Conference to support France's actions. The conference was taking place in New Zealand, the country most concerned about the impact of the French tests. To add insult to injury, at the same time Britain was 'entertaining' seven French warships on a goodwill visit.

Serious questions

Why and how has this environmental insanity arisen? Why do we, in the main, care and do so little about it? Do government and industry understand the gravity of the global environmental catastrophe that is already taking place? Would they tell us if they did? How could we stop the rot or reverse the trend? How much of the damage is already irreversible? How can a caring, concerned person make a difference? What are you or I going to do about it *today*?

There are no simple answers to such questions and the answers that are forthcoming are often quite contradictory – and depend, of course, on which particular political, commercial or environmental axe is on the grindstone at the time. We all know that well-intentioned campaigners are inclined to exaggerate, which energizes some and turns off others. We all know that commercial and political vested interests and investment in the maintenance of the status quo are massive, whether they are sensible or not. We all know how consistently institutional lies are exposed in the end, but institutions still keep telling them.

Recent history

For hundreds of thousands of years homo erectus lived with and in nature in a mutually harmonious way. Through storms, earthquakes, plague and pestilence, nature demonstrated its immense power and earned the awe and respect of the earth's inhabitants. These natural disasters did not prevent many cultures from truly loving their Mother Earth and treating her with godlike reverence, none more so than Native Americans. People have abused and exploited other people throughout our recorded history, but they did not have the means or the power seriously to abuse the earth – until about 150 years ago.

During the millisecond of universal time that has passed since then, we have run amok, driven by **greed**, drunk on our power. We have been on a hydrocarbon binge, draining the vats of vintage, million-year-old stored sunlight, spewing out the excess to foul every corner of our planet. Like every drunk, we have done so in a loud and arrogant manner with never a care for those who share our home, or for the future. Mindless and excessive self-gratification, however, has inevitable consequences, first for others, but ultimately for ourselves.

❏ In the last 50 years more than 75 per cent of the forests in Europe have been severely damaged by acid rain pollution.

❏ The burning associated with the destruction of our tropical forests alone puts 52 billion kilogrammes of carbon dioxide into the atmosphere per year, which equals 40 per cent of the world's industrial emissions.

❏ Every day US farmers draw out 20 billion more gallons of water from the ground than are replaced by rainfall and 25 billion tons of fertile topsoil are lost globally every year.

❏ The average American drives a car, works to buy it, looks after it and so on for 1,600 hours a year. Dividing the mileage covered by the time spent supporting the car gives an average speed of five miles per hour. To attain the speed of a bicycle, we are devastating our cities, air, lungs and lives.

❏ Every American consumes some 35lb of resources a week and 2,000lb of waste is discarded to produce those resources. In Germany, by comparison, the waste figure is 900lb.

❏ Since 1970 the USA has spent over $1 trillion in the control of pollution and hazardous waste and the US environment is more polluted today than it was then.

❏ 25 million people per year, or 48 people per minute, mainly in Third World countries, succumb to the effects of pesticide poisoning.

❏ The rate of species extinction today is between 1,000 and 10,000 times greater than the natural rate of extinction.

These few claims are only the tips of the environmental iceberg. It took little more than one tip to sink the *Titanic* while the crew failed to spot the danger and the passengers partied! How many tips would it take to sink our planet? Are we to play crew or passenger in the drama? And who will take care of the children?

Environmental researchers are obliged to specialize and each finds disturbing evidence in their own field. Each revelation alone is enough to cause great concern, but when the whole spectrum of crises are assembled, the picture reveals nothing less than a global catastrophe in the making. The impact of its breadth, its enormity and its stupidity is liable to stun us into disbelief and inaction. Who is going to take action on our behalf?

Few politicians can afford to raise their sights beyond the next election, even if they wanted to. Long-term bad news is not a good vote catcher. US Vice President Al Gore is a notable exception and his book *Earth in the Balance: Ecology and the Human Spirit* is an important contribution to the environmental debate. The area of concern of the average politician seldom expands beyond the local or national electorate. In addition, no government has yet demonstrated the capacity or the will, or perhaps the detachment, to contend with the vast power of industry, finance and individual self-interest – the collective **greed** of corporate humanity in its *assertion* phase.

The capitalist myth

Blind belief in capitalism increased following the demise of communism. Although Adam Smith's theory had intended better, capitalism is fuelled by **greed** in practice. Expansion, asset stripping, economic growth, high return on investment, takeovers, wealth creation and market forces are the ugly language of short-term gain and of long-term environmental death. The two are, however, converging as the effects of environmental degradation begin to erode not only the soil, but also the profits.

Business, having enjoyed a 150-year hayride, will soon be jolted into realizing that it cannot continue to strip the earth's assets. Once business has stolen everything from future generations, it will begin to eat up its more immediate reserves – and to panic.

The capitalist faithful espouse the view that 'market forces will always balance things out', but they have made a serious miscalculation – they have failed to calculate the true cost of the product. Vast but not so hidden costs have been omitted by a combination of ignorance and false accounting.

> ❑ If, for example, the true costs of nuclear power were calculated, including the full cost of nuclear waste disposal and decommissioning of obsolete power stations, it would be a non-starter.
> ❑ If the timber and paper industries had to cost in the maintenance of the earth's timber resources, to pay for the disposal of waste and to pay for the environmental damage done by their processes and by-products, the price of our furniture and our magazines would quadruple.
> ❑ If motor manufacturers had to pay for every old car to be environmentally disposed of, together with the health costs associated with its manufacture and the use of its products, we would not be replacing our cars every two years.
> ❑ If the agrochemical industry had to pay for the deaths of the 25 million people killed by its products every year, we would soon revert to organic farming.

Who *does* pay for these things? In the main, at the moment anyway, it is the future generations who will pay the dreadful price. A few years ago that would have meant our great-great-great-grandchildren – today it means our children. Don't we care about them?

Procrastination

The feeble attempts we are making at the moment to clean up the mess are insufficient, in fact they are doomed to fail. We neither have the wisdom nor the will to do it. When business is unwilling to inconvenience shareholders in order to meet emission and pollution control standards, it lobbies the government to alleviate the obligation and lower the standards that are already far too low. Governments invariably concede. Britain, under a long-lived Tory administration, now has some of the weakest environmental legislation in Europe. **Greed** has prevailed.

We have to change our thinking. We have to stop imagining that we can produce waste and clean it up. We have proved that we can't. For example, it was calculated in 1986 that if the US chemical industry was forced to incinerate the waste from its top 50 products, it would cost it $100 per ton or $20 billion, eight times its profit in the same year. This is an impossible equation. Instead we must develop non-polluting processes and products. No waste must be the goal. This means a fundamental rethink of business priorities. As the Tomorrow's Company Conference in London suggested, all the stakeholders must have a say and the environment is a stakeholder. In most instances this means that the environment should, and in time will, take priority over the shareholders.

If we think we can't afford the global costs of radical changes to our thinking and the way we run our business, consider this observation by Paul Hawken in his seminal book *The Ecology of Commerce*:

The US and the former USSR spent over $10 trillion on the Cold War, enough money to replace the entire infrastructure of the world, every school, every hospital, every roadway, building and farm. In other words we bought and sold the whole world in order to defeat a political movement. To now assert that we don't have the resources to build a restorative economy is ironic, since the threats we face today are actually happening, whereas the threats of the post-war nuclear stand-off were about the possibility of destruction.

Hope springs eternal

However, there are some positive signs:

- ❏ US conglomerate 3M is a flagship for the merging of environmental and economic interests. In the 15 years which followed the initiation of its Pollution Prevention Pays programme, it saved $537 million, reduced air pollution by 120,000 tons, waste water by a billion gallons and solid waste by 400,000 tons.
- ❏ In the 1970s concern about the toxic effects of vinyl chloride expressed by the US Environmental Protection Agency forced the plastics industry to re-examine its manufacturing methods. The techniques discovered have actually reduced the cost of plastic and reduced the emission of vinyl chloride into the atmosphere down to about 2 per cent of the emissions of 20 years earlier.
- ❏ The tuna fishing industry has been forced to eliminate certain types of net which were causing the deaths of tens of thousands of dolphins every year. By 1992 the number of dolphins killed had fallen to a mere 5 per cent of the figures from five years earlier.
- ❏ With certain exceptions, city air quality in the most developed nations has improved in the past 15 years, with carbon monoxide and sulphur dioxide concentrations dropping by some 30 per cent and lead pollution by 75 per cent. This is the result of a faster than expected switch to unleaded fuel in cars.
- ❏ We are right to deplore the destruction of the rainforests in the Amazon delta, but the forestry news is not all bad. In the US, 600 million acres of forest in 1920 has expanded to 730 million acres today. Papermaking has been a bugbear of environmentalists, but recycling is up and mill processes have improved enormously. For example, in the last 20 years one of the largest mills in the world, at Longview, Washington, has reduced its water emissions by 95 per cent, its solid waste by 25 per cent, its particulate emissions by 80 per cent and its sulphur emissions by 98 per cent. However, its miniscule emission of dioxin attracted the wrath of both the state of Washington and Greenpeace. It is hard to be perfect!

Unfortunately, for every major company like 3M attempting to do the right thing, there are many more that will stop at nothing to satisfy their **greed**. Two-thirds of the Fortune 500 companies were involved in illegal actions between 1975 and 1985, and 115 of them were convicted of a serious crime between 1980 and 1985. Street crime is big business in the US at $5 billion a year, but corporate crime amounts to $50 billion per year. Shocking as this may be, it should be seen in conjunction with the fact that much abhorrent corporate behaviour remains legal thanks to favourable legislation provided by legislators with considerable vested interests. Russia, emerging from the tight controls of communism into *assertion,* is beset with corporate and organized crime which adds fuel to uncontrolled pollution.

A developing problem

The picture that emerges is paradoxical. As a nation passes from agriculture to industrialization, environmental damage occurs on an increasing scale. At a certain point, however, whether brought about by legislation, public pressure, economic expansion, technological advancement or all of the above, the tide of environmental destruction seems to turn back. The factor which underlies all these may well be the evolutionary one. In spite of the highly visible manifestations of *assertion* in the developed world and their environmental consequences, pockets of *cooperation* are just beginning to emerge.

We cannot attribute cause and effect in a system so chaotic that only chaos theory can embrace it – unless we look at it all as just part of human evolution in the macrocosm. At least evolution is inevitable and sequential, so our three-stage model suggests. Bypassing the *assertion* stage, with all its attendant problems, is regrettably not an option.

Speedy evolution through the stages of our simple model cannot be forced or coerced without leaving the potential for problems and reversals. Communism failed disastrously because *cooperation* was imposed, not chosen. People were far from ready to be *cooperative*.

This has not stopped people asking the difficult questions. Should the developed nations assist the developing nations to proceed as quickly as possible through the destructive *assertive* stage, or should we discourage them from embarking on industrial development at all, with its filthy effects for a generation or two? And do the industrial nations have the right to decide or to withhold the necessary economic assistance and technology? Don't 'developing' nations have the right to go through the same development process as we did?

The best hope would seem to be for the developed nations to become good role models, to share their technology for good, and to support the developing nations economically. Of course some of this is happening – but so is economic exploitation, the exercise of power and other behaviours associated with *assertion*. The **greed** and *assertion* of those in the developed West continues to kill both ourselves and those in **need** in other parts of the world.

In spite of my horrible diagnosis, I am optimistic about the prognosis because, after a long enough sleep, we all wake up. I believe that we all want our world to survive and for it to be a better world. I believe that human beings have an incredible capacity for creativity, ingenuity and problem solving, when they need and want to use it. I believe that all human beings are essentially well meaning, good, caring and *cooperative*, beneath their fears, desires and defences. I believe that we can and will save our world from ourselves – just and just in time.

10
National Cooperation

To what extent do the relationships within and between nations reflect the evolutionary trends suggested by our three-stage model? I will cite some examples of international confrontations and *co-operation* from the recent past which suggest that the model not only holds good on a macro scale, but also can help us place apparently irrational behaviours by some nations into a logical context. I may appear to be going walkabout from the field of business which is the principal thrust of this book – but global events are the context in which business takes place, and some business people have found that too much gazing at their VDU screens has limited their vision.

Can we foresee a time in the future when nations will truly *co-operate* to support one another through their difficult times? Can we hope for a reduction in barriers to trade and trust between people and nations, and for an appreciation of differences rather than a suspicion of them? Will the powerful nations always exploit the weaker developing nations as sources of cheap labour and as markets for products that can not be sold at home? How will shifts in the balance between political power and corporate power change the societies in which we live?

United Nations

I can cite a number of examples of international *cooperation* in recent times, beginning with the League of Nations which led to the United Nations. The impulse behind these initiatives was *cooperation* and world peace. Alliances that may ultimately benefit everyone are often founded on self-interest, for example NATO and the old Warsaw Pact were formed for defence purposes, and more recently the European Economic Community and ASEAN (the Association of South East Asian Nations) were established to provide economic power and protection for their members.

We are also experiencing a trend in the opposite direction. Ethnic and historical divisions are reasserting themselves. More breakaway movements are developing, and ever more countries are being formed. The more obvious ones have arisen through the break-up of the former Soviet Union and Yugoslavia, but there are many others. Did you know, for example, that Andorra, a small enclave of 47,000 people sandwiched between France and Spain, is now a country in its own right with a seat in the United Nations?

The United Nations was a bold attempt to raise the flag of international *cooperation*, but it has fallen far short of our hopes and its promises, nowhere more tragically than in the Balkans. The peace-keepers who were there in the main performed a difficult task well, given their limited brief and resources, but they were powerless to prevent appalling massacres and inhuman behaviour. The news is not all bad. The fact that the UN still exists is something of a miracle, and, given the diversity of its many constituent countries and cultures, we should acknowledge that it has, at times, demonstrated remarkable feats of *cooperation*.

European Union

The concept behind the European Union was *cooperation*. Like most progressive ideas, it was conceived with good intentions but in the bed of old *assertive* habits, mistrust, control, self interest etc, so it was far from perfect at birth. Most thinking people realize that a wider European community is an essential next step in social evolution towards a world of reduced barriers and mistrust. However, some ultra-conservative British politicians, whose interest is confined to 'our own island patch', our sovereignty, and whose autonomy and *assertive* values are threatened by the idea of European *cooperation*, are fighting a vigorous rearguard action. In the long term they will fail, but they have forced the government into the worst possible compromise. Britain is standing in the doorway to Europe making ill-conceived and self-serving demands to satisfy internal critics rather than to contribute, thereby frustrating the more committed European partners and further damaging the prospects for a *cooperative* Europe.

The fall of The Wall

The demise of the Soviet Union and the breaching of the Berlin Wall are unquestionably seen as having produced the greatest change on the world stage in the last half century. Once the process began, the speed at which it all happened took everyone by surprise. Suddenly the communist threat which we had been told was hanging over our heads was lifted. Almost overnight the principle evaporated for the CIA in the United States, the KGB in the Soviet Union and MI5 in Britain, for the vast and excessive array of nuclear weapons and for the endless propaganda overkill by both sides. In the celebration of the end of the 45-year stand-off, it is easy to forget the carnage committed by both sides in smaller countries who had little choice but to align, to die switching sides or to die attempting to remain non-aligned.

Wars by proxy

I could list the 44 minor wars, from Korea to Nicaragua, fought out by the old superpowers on Third World pitches, using local troops equipped with horrendous modern weaponry. The players and their families, who were abandoned and forgotten by the sponsors after the game, are now dead or maimed without the wherewithal for medical, environmental or economic recovery. Five million dead is a conservative estimate, and less than a tenth of them Russians and Americans.

The tonnage of bombs dropped by the United States on a 250-mile-wide strip of Cambodia in a nine-month period exceeded the tonnage of bombs dropped by both sides during the whole of the

Second World War. Agent Orange, a US chemical weapon used osten-
sibly to clear foliage, is still causing tragic birth defects in Vietnam.
The excuse the Americans used to initiate the biggest escalation of the
Vietnam War, the Gulf of Tonkin incident, was pure fabrication. US
sponsorship of Contra terrorists against Nicaragua, and arms and
training support to the brutal military dictatorships of Guatemala and
El Salvador in the 1970s and 1980s, were ill-conceived, wrong-head-
ed interventions steeped in blood and devoid of justification. I saw it;
I was there.

No winners

So much has been written about Soviet crimes in the former
Czechoslovakia, Hungary, Afghanistan and in small countries which
they had previously devoured like Latvia and Estonia, as well as the
suppression of their own people, that there is no need to repeat it all
here. In the aftermath of the Cold War neither side comes out with
any credit. The outcome and the failure of the Soviet communist
regime should not be confused with the intent and the means with
which the 'war' was conducted. There were no winners, but a huge
number of largely innocent losers.

What, if anything, has humanity learned from this? Certainly the
paranoia that was rife on both sides has gone. Russia is, and will be
for some time, consumed with shoring up its own economic stability,
and the United States is the last remaining superpower. US responses
to international crises under President Clinton are now far more
measured.

It may be illuminating to consider the period from the Russian revolution to the demise of the Soviet Union in terms of our three-stage
model.

If our western post-industrial information society is clearly still in
the *assertion* phase of evolution, where was the Soviet Union while it
was a superpower, and where is what is left of it now? The *inclusion*
or invasion phase occurred by force in 1917 and at various times
thereafter. The internal *assertion* phase was never allowed to take
place, as it would have exposed the leaders to the risk of individual

expression and probably challenges to the leadership itself. Instead, Lenin and his 'brothers' imposed a Marxist vision of a *cooperative* society on their people. Thwarting the natural evolutionary course and bypassing *assertion* for coerced *cooperation* meant that true *cooperation* could never be reached. Even the appearances of it could only be achieved or sustained by totalitarian tyranny. The *inclusion* parameters had been imposed, so remained unresolved, but it was the *assertion* needs of ordinary people that built up and eventually burst out first in the Soviet satellites and then in the Soviet Union itself.

The demise of the Soviet system was predictable and inevitable because the laws of evolution had been violated. The collapse of the Soviet Union and of communism was not so much a failure of a wrong political system, but a socio-evolutionary necessity. Repressed *assertion* needs had built up a head of steam over years. Information from abroad, failures from within, corruption arising from the unrequited *assertive* **greed** of the controlling class and the emergence of a visionary leader, Gorbachev, converged and the breakdown occurred. As a moderate reformer Gorbachev was sacrificed in the rush to grab western *assertive* ways, and the more radical Yeltsin swept to power on public euphoria.

Of course it was all too good to be true, the honeymoon was soon over and the collapse continued. I suspect Gorbachev's medicine would have proved less tasty, but the patient might not have suffered such a complete relapse. However, 73 years of repression cannot be swept aside without a major disruption to the system. It imploded and fell into near chaos. Organized crime, profiteering, drugs and vice, all so commonplace in *assertive* capitalist societies, ran riot. *Inclusion* concerns resurfaced while the fires of *assertion* still burned bright. Old countries reformed and new ones were carved out. Almost immediately conflicts between them arose. The Russians who lived in Estonia and Latvia now faced *inclusion* issues. Russia and the Ukraine argued as to how to divide up the Soviet fleet and the nuclear missiles on Ukrainian territory. And the Azeris and Armenians raised the flags of *inclusion* and *assertion* by fighting over 'their' territory in which 'the others' lived. Chechnya's bid for independence was a disaster for Russia and for Chechnya. For those countries and cultures who used to comprise the Soviet Union the socio-evolutionary game of snakes and ladders continues.

If we look at theoretical communism in a charitable light, it can be seen as a visionary attempt to create an ideal society. In practice, and on this occasion, it failed dismally. Self-congratulatory comparisons with our western society then or now should not be made with over-confidence.

In 1979, long before the collapse, my wife and I visited Moscow at a time when the Soviet Union was being portrayed as especially threatening and Americans were seeing a Red under every bed. We went on a civilian diplomacy peace initiative engaged in unofficial Soviet–American scientific exchanges. There we moved around freely, without the accompanying KGB Intourist guide we had been warned to expect. A Soviet scientist told me a personal story that I never forgot. It taught me just how much we are blinded by our own propaganda and the selective criteria we employ.

The Russian had visited Washington on a scientific mission a year or two earlier. On arrival at his hotel, he had decided to go for a stroll in the city. The hotel manager hastily counselled him not to do so because 'it is not safe to walk around here after six o'clock in the evening'. The Russian had been deeply shocked. 'You present yourself as the country of the free,' he had said, 'and I cannot even go out of my hotel for fear of my life. What kind of freedom is this?' In those days it was possible to walk anywhere in Moscow at any time of night without giving a thought to one's personal safety, as indeed my wife and I did.

A Russian woman, who was no supporter of the horrible regime, also helped me to wake up. Not long before, in Miami, several black youths had been shot and killed by the police during rioting. She read about it in a news magazine that I had brought with me. She remarked quite casually that if Russian civilians had been shot on the streets of Moscow by their police, it would have been headlined by the US media and used as a major propaganda coup. She was, of course, absolutely right.

Setback

Unfortunately the world-wide collapse of communism has unjustifiably set back the belief in the possibility of large-scale social *cooperation*. The spectacular failure of the Soviet Union is seen by some as proof that the western way of capitalist *assertion* is right. Even Marxists themselves feel badly let down, and that their cause is tarnished by the Soviet Union's bad example and failure.

Prompted by the Soviet experience and the world's revulsion at the appalling events of Tiananmen Square, the Chinese seem to be trying to open up and become capitalist fast enough to avoid a Soviet-style collapse. For decades they have imposed the same coercion to *cooperate* and the same need for *assertion* is bubbling underneath. The Chinese do not face the problem the Soviets had in the form of an opposing superpower, but they have internal problems with Tibet and thorny issues with Hong Kong and Taiwan. They probably won't succeed, but the jury is still out.

Western assertion

In the West, *assertion* values are so deeply entrenched in business, industry and government, which serve as our role models, that few of us ever think to question them. The criteria of success and status demand that we be *assertive*. Rewards are given in our society for acts that exemplify *assertion*, not *cooperation*. The organizational structure, the hierarchy, the rewards and the punishments of our institutions of government, business, education and training, sport and even leisure and social services, the very structure of our social fabric, if not designed by *assertive* people is sustained by them for their own kind.

The *assertion* stage is seductive with its currency of material goods, indulgence and extravagance, stimulation, gratification of desire, power, display and macho, all stuff which appeals to our earthly humanness. Meeting these desires, and convincing us that we need even more of them, enables business to tick along very nicely doing more of what it already does, and earning more profit from it.

Early signs

There are signs of continuing progress towards *cooperation* – but despite our efforts, not because of them. In fact, many of those signs are appearing internationally through multinational corporations, some through necessity, some through design. In the motor industry, for example, there are a number of transnational *cooperative* pairings between erstwhile competitors, such as BMW and Rover, Ford and Nissan, Volkswagen and Skoda. Some but by no means all of these end up as mergers. There are those changes, such as delayering, team-building, shared responsibility, coaching and self-motivation, which collectively we have called fundamental business culture change. Transnational environmental initiatives are another example, whether driven by ecology evangelists or essential or emergency Eurolegislation.

Businesses or individuals with enough vision to read the writing on the wall are not waiting for events to push them reluctantly towards *cooperation*. They are initiating the movement themselves, thereby remaining in control of their own evolving destiny. This is how our society is changing, not through any great world leader, not through the doctrine of any great ideologue, not through any one country leading the way, but through pockets of progressive people every-where. Business people have a big part to play in this – if they want to play.

Leadership

So what role does leadership have in this change? Leaders in business or in government are always expected to be *assertive*. The saying that what one has to do to get into a high place makes one unworthy of that position will become ever more true. It is not easy or pleasant for someone who has fully embraced *cooperation* to play the *assertion* game hard enough in an *assertive* world to get to the top – and would they want to? Leaders with a genuine *cooperative* philosophy are rare, and their tenure is often short.

Mahatma Gandhi blended leadership with *cooperation* in a saintly way. Others attempted to emulate him, such as Martin Luther King, who lived and died with the paradox. Bobby Kennedy, Mikhail Gorbachev, Allende of Chile, Ortega of Nicaragua and others experienced varying degrees of success at coping with the contradictions between their personal beliefs and what their roles demanded of them. All fell, and all are still subject to strong but often contradictory judgements by people from opposing sides of the *assertion/ cooperation* divide.

Another great statesman was projected on the world stage out of Africa, Nelson Mandela. He is a visionary who exemplifies Gandhian qualities such as dignity, tenacity, humility, forgiveness and *cooperation*. He is perhaps the only major national leader in the world today worthy of the title of statesman, although there are other less well-known figures who display similar qualities, such as Burmese dissident Aung San Suu Kyi or the Dali Lama.

Thatcherism

Margaret Thatcher was a role model for *assertion*. With an infuriating brand of matronizing autocracy, she attempted to coerce us all into being more self-reliant and self-responsible – an admirable and evolutionary concept, but forcing people to be more responsible is an unworkable contradiction which is usually closely followed by blame when they fail. What was needed was a more supportive government policy to create the conditions in which people could, and would, choose self-responsibility and succeed. What did we get instead?

The rule of the marketplace, the competitive commercial world, consumerism, **greed** being condoned if not encouraged, and education, health, welfare and essential services being deprived of necessary funding, cut or privatized. The **greed** of the winners was rewarded, and the **needs** and dependence of the more numerous losers were increased.

By now the ship was trimmer, but the crew was disenchanted and some of the ship's officers mutinied. Captain Thatcher was forced to walk the plank. An uninspiring steward took the helm in an atmosphere of optimism, but he had no major vision. His lieutenants had none either, so they threw their weight around so indiscriminately and scandalously that damage limitation seemed to be their only consistent policy. An anti-European, anti-*cooperation* faction grew on the right of the party. The result: the government and its new leader lost all credibility and the public was further alienated.

Socialism with a new face, Tony Blair's, seems ever more attractive and begins to look like embryo *cooperation*. It remains to be seen if the New Labour Party or the Social Democrats will do any better socially, nationally or within Europe, but at least the words of Blair and Ashdown are cause for cautious optimism. Could they not *co-operate* with each other? Time will tell if their words are based on a true long-term vision of where our society and our civilization are going – *cooperation*.

An example extinguished

There are no examples of *cooperative* blocs of countries, or even single countries, that I can cite with safety. But there have been signs of *cooperation* in Scandinavia, in New Zealand and in Israel when under threat. And Nicaragua under threat was positively inspiring. My visit there in 1984 coincided with the celebration of the fifth anniversary of the overthrow of the brutal Somoza dictatorship. The atmosphere almost everywhere was euphoric, and the commitment of ordinary people to building a new, fair society was extraordinary. The peasant literacy programme, the healthcare initiatives, the redistribution of land, the open prison policy and liberation theology were models of inclusiveness and *cooperation*. But large landowners and business people, a small minority who had benefited under Somoza, were disadvantaged and disaffected – and they had friends in the United States.

The Sandinista peasant revolution had huge potential, but it was systematically destroyed from without by the US economic embargo and US-sponsored terrorism, and from within by these remnants of the disenfranchised oligarchy. At that time the United States, paranoid about anything that had a whiff of communism, could not tolerate having a successful left-leaning, pluralist, *cooperative* society in its own backyard. Today under Clinton, and with the Soviet Union gone, the Sandinistas would have qualified for full US support; if they had had the benefit of this at the time they might have become a model for national *cooperation*. Unfortunately history can not be rewritten and too much of the Nicaraguan spark of greatness has been extinguished.

Cooperation that sustains at a national or international level at a time when there is little external threat to force people to set aside their differences will be a long time coming. It should, however, be a permanent part of any vision of the future.

Of course, this is all far from simple. Nowhere in history can we find any obvious examples of truly *cooperative* large societies. Most cultures eventually tear themselves apart in the *assertion* stage and have to start all over again.

A small Scottish example

However, pockets of people have emerged from time to time all over the world which have aspired to *cooperation*. They have come in many different forms. Kibbutzim in Israel are an example, as are Easterhouse in Scotland, Mondragon in Spain, the Cooperative movement, and even early in the 19th century Robert Owen, an enlightened capitalist who built a model factory and community with its own housing, welfare system and a factory school in Lanarkshire, Scotland.

The ethos in Scotland has long been one of democracy and community, which is perhaps why it is the home of one of the most inspirational communities I know. At Findhorn, near Inverness, a community came together in the 1960s which is a micro model of what a *cooperative* society of the future might look like. Findhorn is not perfect – it has its neuroses and failures and makes mistakes just like the rest of us – but it has passed through *inclusion*, it has survived a few rocky *assertion* periods and it is more often now in *cooperation*. It will have more breakdowns and more breakthroughs before it is done.

Findhorn has gradually expanded over the years and today is the home for some 350 people of many nationalities and creeds. It has a profoundly spiritual base but is non-denominational. It is a learning and teaching organization, with an active global outreach. Findhorn has had several vision statements along a similar theme, but the following is perhaps the most illustrative:

> We are a spiritual centre of transformation, education, healing and demonstration, working with the qualities of love and wisdom to embody a vision of God, humanity and nature in co-creation and thereby offering hope, vision, inspiration and encouragement.

Sound ecology has always been central to the organization of the community's physical space. The famed 40lb cabbages from its early organic gardens defied rational explanation, as evidenced by this comment made in 1969 by Professor Robb of the Soil Association:

> The vigour, health and bloom of the plants in this garden at midwinter on land which is almost barren, powdery sand, can not be explained by the moderate dressings of compost, nor indeed by the application of any known cultural methods of organic husbandry. There are other factors at work and they are vital ones.

Findhorn is currently creating at its centre a model eco-village with which to demonstrate sustainability and ecological balance. The coordinator of the project describes the eco-houses they are building as 'the 40lb cabbages of the 1990s'.

Findhorn anticipates an imminent transformation, in my terms from *assertion* to *cooperation*. A clause in the Findhorn Foundation Trust Deed states that its work is based on 'the belief that humanity is on the verge of a major evolutionary step which can be achieved through a change in consciousness' and Findhorn actively works towards creating that change. It provides a role model as well as a practical outreach to assist others to develop and maintain *cooperative* communities all over the world.

11
Ego Boundaries

At this point I am going to introduce another model of individual and social development to provide a second perspective on our evolutionary journey. It is intended to be complementary rather than an alternative to the three-stage model we are examining. This model shows how an individual's sphere of interest or area of concern, sometimes described as ego boundaries, expands with their psychological evolution or personal development.

In order not to overcomplicate the diagram I have only indicated three areas, geographical, people and work. Of course our ego boundaries restrict the extent of our vision and concern about many other aspects of life, but these serve to illustrate the point.

Babyhood boundaries

A newborn baby's first concern, subconscious of course, is for its own survival. For this he (or she) needs nourishment and he soon makes himself heard when breast or bottle is required. His comfort or shelter and safety are also loudly called for, and usually willingly provided by his parents. During the initial stage of life, his area of concern could be said to be solely himself.

The provision of comfort blends with bonding with the mother, and hopefully the father too, which is the first part of belonging or *inclusion*. Before long the baby will show signs of conscious recognition of his mother, and the mother's moods may influence those of the baby. His area of concern now begins to include his nearest and dearest. The family is the first unit to which the baby belongs. His ego boundaries have begun to expand to include mum and dad. Orphans

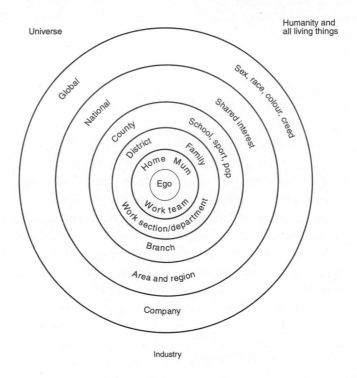

Figure 8: The ego boundary model

from birth who are not given very special individual care and attention are completely deprived of the opportunity to meet their earliest belonging needs and may suffer psychological damage as a result.

Childhood boundaries

As the young child develops, his 'living' stuffed animals and dolls are *included* in his area of concern. The child becomes concerned for their well-being and may attempt to feed them as well as lovingly pulling their heads off! Brothers and sisters begin to fall into his areas of interest. His ego boundaries now include his immediate animate and inanimate family. By the time many children are two years old, the first of several cycles of *assertion* may have begun alongside the *inclusion* needs. This is known as the terrible twos – although, as most parents know, it lasts forever!

Adolescent boundaries

In time the child will develop attachments to playmates, school friends and a few pop or sports stars and acquire some sense of belonging to a locality. He may support Manchester United or the Dallas Cowboys and speak of them as 'we', indicating that 'they' are now included in his ego boundaries. In adolescence, notably in areas where young people are deprived of quality family life, belonging to a gang, usually one with a territory to defend, or becoming a skinhead, punk, mod, rocker or even a teddy boy of old, is important if not imperative. The adolescent's ego boundaries divides 'us' from 'them' outside. To *inclusion* is added a further dose of *assertion*.

Locality boundaries

People of all ages will identify with a locality. It may be a town or just a few streets in an area with a pub at each corner. It may be the county or state whose sports teams they support, but it is also what is called home, to be defended against foreigners or critics from other 'inferior' counties or states. It will encompass their place of work, but not necessarily the head office of the business if it is located further afield. It is territory with which they feel familiar and within which they feel safe.

National boundaries

Many adults never expand their ego boundaries much further than this. Sports teams change in little but name, school mates become workmates, gangs become special interest groups, clubs, political parties or trade unions. Their individual social evolution or maturing slows or stops. National boundaries are the limit of many people's ego boundaries, notably certain right-wing politicians and Alf Garnett types. Even to those who frequently go on holiday abroad, foreigners will always remain 'them'. Nationalism can easily turn Nazi!

Others, however, develop interests further afield. They tire of tabloid titillation and try reading *Time* magazine instead. They take an interest in current affairs, in Round Table, Rotary or professional associations with some outreach, in international sport and in global events.

Ego boundaries at work

For some people, their area of concern at work only encompasses their immediate workmates; it may be their section, their own team, their open-plan office or their floor in the building; it may be their function, IT, sales, manufacturing or the service department; it may be their branch or their site out of the three at which the company operates; it may be the company as a whole or beyond to commercial sectors, such as the financial services sector or the motor trade.

Staff and employees will tend to limit their personal aspirations to the area one step larger than their immediate area of concern or identification. They will be aware of the larger area, but only feel responsible for their own. The outer limit of a person's area of awareness is sometimes seen as the limit of their potential for promotion. This is not a good yardstick because all people can expand their horizons hugely if they make a conscious choice to do so, if they feel safe enough or if circumstances force them to.

If and when a person's ego boundaries or area of concern become global, their perspective on work may change. They may see their work more as a contribution to society, more than as an end in itself. They may be dedicated and work hard but they know that the world of work is only another piece in the game of life, that it has little intrinsic importance. They are not attached to or in deep need of their work. While they may remain fiercely loyal to their employer, their ultimate higher allegiance, should conflicting imperatives reveal themselves, will be to society, not to the company. Contrary to what some employers might fear, such people are generally the most productive and work to the highest personal standards. This, of course, parallels the area of *cooperation* and relates also to Maslow's self-actualizer's need for meaning and purpose.

Expanding boundaries

Some people's ego boundaries never really stop expanding, particularly those who have opportunities, feel more secure or are naturally inquisitive. They become more concerned about the suffering in Rwanda, the fate of whales or the destruction of the rainforests than they are about local issues which may actually affect them more personally. It is not uncommon once this stage has been reached for people to seek work directly related to their area of global concern. They have moved fully into the stage of *cooperation* with the greater whole. Their area of concern and ego boundaries now embrace the world, but expansion does not necessarily stop there.

The discussion which follows identifies some of the areas beyond the geophysical boundaries of our planet in which there has been an upsurge in interest in the past 30 or 40 years. Just as our three-stage model applies to individuals and to groups of all sizes, so does the ego boundary model. Although the areas listed below now have a higher profile, it does not imply that all those who are interested or involved in these things have expanded their personal boundaries to that extent. Most of us end up displaying a confusing mixture of concerns related to the size of our personal ego boundaries, the boundaries of the macro groups which most influence us and a band at the leading edge of our collective ego boundaries.

Space exploration

From the 1960s onwards there has been a growing interest in a number of strangely connected areas. There was space travel, culminating in men on the moon and probes to Mars and beyond. Hubble's distant revelations and the exploration of space generated vast public interest, but could it also be said that the public's growing interest in space enabled space exploration to occur? Astronauts who had looked at Earth from a great distance have consistently said that they saw whole continents but none of the barriers and boundaries that are the primary cause of conflict. I include a few of their comments here:

> For those who have seen Earth from space, the experience certainly changes your perspective. The things that we share in our world are more valuable than those that divide us. (Donald Williams, USA)
>
> From space I saw Earth, indescribably beautiful, with the scars of national boundaries gone. (Muhammad Ahmad Faris, Syria)
>
> After an orange cloud – formed as a result of a dust storm over the Sahara and caught up by air currents – reached the Philippines and settled there with rain, I understood that we are all sailing in the same boat. (Vladimir Kovalyonok, USSR)
>
> And then it struck me that we are all children of our Earth. It does not matter what country you look at. We are all Earth's children, and we should treat her as our Mother. (Aleksandr Aleksandrov, USSR)

The astronautical perspective on the next page was created in a novel way by an unnamed soul who cared for our Earth in a way that we all can and will when we transcend the limits of our personal ego boundaries.

Science fiction

Then came the burgeoning field of science fiction literature and films. There were children's space cartoons from Buck Rogers to Dan Dare and more recently video games from Space Invaders to Doom. There was Arthur C. Clarke's appropriately named book *Childhood's End* and Stanley Kubrick's amazing film *2001*, still one of the greats. *Star*

If the Earth
were   only   a   few   feet   in
diameter, floating   a   few   feet   above
a   field   somewhere,   people   would   come
from everywhere to marvel at it. People would
walk around it, marvelling at its big pools of water,
its little pools and the water flowing between the pools.
People would marvel at the bumps on it, and the holes in it,
and they would marvel at the very thin layer of gas surrounding
it and the water suspended in the gas. The people would
marvel at all the creatures walking around the surface of the ball,
and at the creatures in the water. The people would declare it
as sacred because it was the only one, and they would protect
it so that it would not be hurt. The ball would be the
greatest wonder known, and people would come to
pray to it, to be healed, to gain knowledge, to know
beauty and to wonder how it could be. People
would love it, and defend it with their lives
because they would somehow know that
their lives, their own roundness, could
be   nothing   without   it.   If   the
Earth   were   only   a   few
feet in diameter.

Trek, which ran to 76 television episodes and four feature films and is still growing in popularity, was the first attempt at presenting at least some of the aliens as non-threatening. *ET* made one of them irresistible. The *Star Wars* series introduced us to the Force, a decidedly religious concept. The London stage musical *Time* had godly overtones, as did the amazingly popular film *Close Encounters of the Third Kind*, which also merged science fiction with UFOs. 1996 was the year of alien autopsies, *The X Files* and *Independence Day*, and there will be much more to come.

UFOs

The interest in unidentified flying objects has been growing ever since 1947 when an American private pilot, Kenneth Arnold, saw something which he described as a flying saucer. There are literally thousands of books of anecdotes and research attesting to the notion that something is definitely going on out there. The majority of ordinary people today believe that governments know more about this than they are sharing with us. The strange and secret goings on at Groom Lake in Nevada and the large number of reported alien abductions in recent years attract investigators and conspiracy theorists in droves. There is much speculation that the US, British and other governments, no longer able to limit and control what the public digs up, have finally decided to orchestrate a programme of misinformation and controlled leaks as a prelude to letting us know that we are not alone in the universe. And then there is the strange phenomenon of crop circles . . .

Subtle energies

At the same time interest in astrology, psychic abilities, synchronicity, dowsing, channelling, past lives, parapsychology and spiritual healing have grown. Homeopathy, osteopathy, acupuncture, chiropractic, aromatherapy and many other forms of complementary medicine are gaining customers, success and respectability. With the help of endorsements by princes and academics, medical orthodoxy and even the British National Health Service and the American Medical Association are having to accommodate rather than eliminate this arena of often scientifically unexplainable effects. The notion that there are forces, often benevolent ones, beyond our ken can no longer be simplistically dismissed by Christians as the work of the devil, as has been the case for centuries. Although all these occurrences will before long be explained within the expanding parameters of science, for the moment they are still regarded by many people as out of this world – and fascinating!

Fundamentals

Although church attendance in Britain and the rest of Europe is still in decline, a rather unsavoury fundamentalist religious revival began in the 1960s. The evangelical movement in the US grew exponentially until **greed** and sleaze forced the converts to recognize that there are plenty of slippery slopes on the road to heaven. And Islamic fundamentalism, of which many of us had previously been barely aware, exploded into our lives in ways which were far from heavenly. At the same time, one of the barriers that Israel has to overcome on the road to peace and eventual *cooperation* in Palestine is the *assertiveness* of the fundamentalist Jewish settlers who are also in the ascendant. Unfortunately, religious fanatics of every creed project the human desire for control on to God. Nevertheless, despite the dreadful distortions and the ugly *assertiveness* of fanatacism, pervasive religious influence may be seen as another manifestation of collective ego boundaries extending beyond our physical world.

Gurus

In the 1960s, eastern gurus acquired many followers from the West looking for meaning beyond their limited egos, and some rich pickings from those anxious to divest themselves of the burden of their material possessions. Not all gurus were as devoid of spirituality as the popular press would have us believe, and what emerged for many people from that time was a journey beyond the narrow confines of any one religion and orthodoxy. The external God of the West and the God within of the East were found not to be mutually exclusive. People began to synthesize their own unique blend of wisdom from many sources, from Buddhism, Hinduism, Islam (particularly from the Sufis), Judaism (particularly from the Kabbalists), from Hopi Indians and from Christian mysticism.

The coincidence of all these recent examples of widespread interest in areas beyond our mundane outer and inner experience are signposts of the collective evolutionary expansion of our ego boundaries. When we expand our ego boundaries to include every living thing in the universe, we are in total *cooperation* with life. This ideal to which we may aspire will always seem just out of reach. But in aspiring towards it we find peace, grace and freedom. This sounds like a spiritual message, but it is also a profoundly psychological one.

Awareness leads to responsibility

Of course, the boundary of the ego, or limit of the area of concern, is not sharply defined. Outside it is innocence or ignorance, not in a pejorative sense but as a vast area of unknown nothingness, rather like outer space appears to most of us. A baby who is by now clearly aware of mum could be said to be totally innocent and ignorant about countries and governments. At the outer limit of the ego boundary is a vague sense of the existence of things, but they are largely ignored. Closer to the centre the definition of the ego boundary becomes firmer or more solid with the beginning of <u>awareness</u>, which involves recognition and retention in the consciousness.

<u>Awareness</u> itself is a huge spectrum which ranges from superficial information about high-profile facts to a vast array of detail, subtlety, interplay and understanding. Refined <u>awareness</u> includes the self-<u>awareness</u> without which our own biases are not recognized and our perception and understanding of other people and things are limited or distorted. Self-<u>awareness</u> at the most refined level acknowledges the subtle influence which the act of observation itself may have on what is observed.

As <u>awareness</u> increases so does interest. It is a vast oversimplification to say that people who are more aware are interested in more things, or in the same things in more depth, but as a general rule it holds true. Accompanying but following on from interest is often the wish beneficially to influence things in which we are interested. This in turn develops into a growing sense of <u>responsibility</u>, leading to action. The injunction that we should 'think globally but act locally' begins to make a lot of sense. We need to understand the big picture, but take action in areas within the reach of our ability and sphere of influence.

Take the example of someone who discovers that her employer is allowing factory effluent to pollute a stream. Before it was ignorance, now it becomes superficial <u>awareness</u> which may lead to interest. That interest, if the person's ego boundaries continue to expand, will begin to include things like the effects of the pollution on the fish in the stream, on human health, on the river into which the stream flows. By this time our employee will have developed some concern and will probably want to influence the situation. If her attempts to influence her boss to stop the pollution are thwarted, she may begin to take more <u>responsibility</u> on her own shoulders, risk her job and become a whistle blower. At this point she is likely to be developing a wider, even global concern for water pollution, which may in turn lead to campaigning over the water of our whole planet – a far cry from the trickle of effluent that started the process.

Many people – including me, in spite of being half Norwegian – are more concerned about cruelty to whales and preservation of the whale species than we are about the Norwegian economy or the livelihood of the few whaling communities. We are driven by the impulse for the *cooperation* of all humanity, and to us the Norwegians seem to be *asserting* their patch. They are banding together in *cooperation* with one another, but within their national ego boundaries.

Anti-Vietnam war activism in the 1960s in the US was a potent example of this issue. The older generation, developmentally limited to national concerns and national ego boundaries and fearful of those subhuman 'commies' out there, regarded the protest movement in part as an avoidance of <u>responsibility</u>. The youthful protesters regarded the older establishment as irresponsible for not including the Vietnamese in their wider area of concern and <u>responsibility</u>.

So each expansion of our ego boundaries begins with an <u>awareness</u> of and interest in issues less connected to our personal lives, followed a little later by a corresponding growth of caring or concern. As we become more <u>aware</u> or better informed, so our sense of wider personal <u>responsibility</u> for everything around us grows. The expansion of our concern is often thwarted by feelings of individual powerlessness in the face of the might of national governments or multinational corporations, whose collective self-interest overrides the wider global social or environmental issues for which we may be developing a concern.

When responsibility (power) exceeds awareness

It is unfortunately not uncommon, particularly where large power blocs are involved such as superpowers or large corporations and also individual dictators, for the expansion to occur in the reverse order. Their sphere of influence and power expands faster than their sphere of <u>awareness</u>, and the exercise of that power in an <u>awareness</u> vacuum is dangerous because that vacuum quickly fills with exaggerated fantasies. The most obvious example of this was during the Cold War when the United States was so poorly informed about the USSR that it demonized the Soviets, exaggerated their power and the threat they constituted. Americans feared their own fantasies rather than the reality. This in turn caused the US to behave aggressively across the globe in the very same manner that it perceived the USSR to be doing. Likewise, the Soviets were very poorly informed about the West and also reacted out of fear and paranoia.

With both sides projecting demonic fantasies on to each other, they came close to blowing the planet away. It is very dangerous when the power circle is larger than the <u>awareness</u> circle. Only when our ego boundaries expand to global proportions and we are able to cast off our nationalistic blinkers do we begin to recognize how often our country's political ambitions and military exploits abroad were calculated acts of *assertion* and self-interest. They were a far cry from heroic national sacrifice in defence of a weaker neighbour, which is the way they are presented to us by our government or our jingoistic tabloid press.

Doesn't the same thing occur in the workplace all the time? I suspect that few business leaders have <u>awareness</u> commensurate with the power they wield. However, before I confront my boss, I would do well to consider how <u>aware</u> I appear to those over whom I exert power.

We must all ensure that our <u>awareness</u> remains a step or two ahead of our area of <u>responsibility</u>. If our field of <u>awareness</u> is very much greater than our sphere of influence or <u>responsibility</u>, we may feel intensely frustrated and disempowered.

Evolution

This raises another perspective of the ego boundary model which parallels the three-stage model of *inclusion, assertion* and *cooperation*. Just as the area of concern of individuals tends to expand along with maturity, so each generation tends to be more mentally expansive than the last. In the business world younger staff often display broader <u>awareness</u> and greater social concern than their senior managers, which can be unsettling for both. We have seen how successive generations tend to develop broader ego boundaries than the last, and how concern for the global environment and about deprivation and cruelty world-wide are examples of the wider *cooperation* consciousness that is emerging everywhere.

In 1972 Senator McGovern opposed Richard Nixon in the US presidential election. Although McGovern lost ignominiously, his best campaign quote was remembered long after his demise and proved to be remarkably apposite: 'What is right has always been called radical by those with a stake in what is wrong.'

The ideas of progressive thinkers today, and even the demands of protest movements currently regarded as beyond the fringe, will in time become mainstream consciousness. The wisdom of collective hindsight will always recognize the validity of wider areas of concern. So it was with the abolition of slavery, the emancipation of women, trade unionism, the environment, racial desegregation and even consumer protection, all forcefully opposed as wrong headed by the establishment initially, but eventually proved to be right. Unfortunately some protesters, driven by force of circumstance, by emotion or by conscious choice, have behaved very *assertively* (aggressively) on the part of causes which are clearly *cooperative* in nature. This contradiction rarely goes unnoticed by those opposing the cause, and the credibility and success of the protest usually suffer – but only for a while.

12
Personal Growth and Spirituality

For most people, growth is a purely physical phenomenon. We reach optimum height in our late teens and only our girth grows thereafter. What this chapter discusses has nothing to do with size, and little to do with age. It is psychological growth, sometimes described as maturing. Many of us think that this is something that just happens as we get older and there is nothing we can do about it. It is assumed to be outside our control, a product of life experience – but is it?

Growth Centres

In the adventurous 1960s Growth Centres sprang up, starting in California and later spreading throughout Europe. These might be described as psychological health farms to which people could retreat for anything from a weekend to a year or more. All manner of group psychotherapies were on offer, some of which drew on meditation, yoga and martial arts techniques from Eastern cultures and others were the products of experimental psychologists working at the outer limits of conventional western psychology.

The attendees at such places were not, as one might expect, schizophrenic, psychotic, paranoid or neurotic but perfectly sane, often successful, people who sought more from life than the mundane. Like everyone they had their psychological hang-ups, but they went there to seek inner riches that money can not buy. Of course, like health farms, growth centres were expensive, and were seen by some as a middle-class luxury or escape. Given the desire, however, the less well off often managed to get there by joining the community staff to work in the grounds by day and on their psyches by night.

While there were undoubtedly some casualties in those heady days, many people grew and expanded themselves psychologically, sometimes quite dramatically. It was not uncommon for attendees to make major changes in their lifestyle and their occupation as a result of their experiences. Although this often caused fear and confusion among family and friends who now saw a different person, the individual experienced new depths and maturity, and the adoption of more meaningful values, often at odds with convention.

To some cultures (for example the British) group psychotherapy is something weird that goes on behind closed doors for criminals, addicts or nutters. To others (such as Americans) growth groups are much more acceptable and accessible and offer normal people opportunities for self-development. Whether we like it or not, we are moving in the American direction. We are becoming less uptight and beginning to own our own emotions. Post-traumatic stress disorder is something to be acknowledged and treated, rather than pushed under the carpet or shot for, as occurred in the First World War. Psychological principles are being more widely applied in sport and in the workplace.

The three stages

It was Dr Will Schutz, one of the fathers of encounter group therapy, who first identified three discrete stages, almost identical to those in our three-stage model, through which a group had to evolve before deep psychological work could be productively undertaken: inclusion, power and control, and affection. Only when the group had reached the *cooperation* or affection stage, as Schutz called it, did the participants trust one another enough to be open and honest, to be intimate, to expose their vulnerabilities, and to take the psychological risks on which successful therapy depends.

Group therapy leaders have to be skilled at moving the group as quickly as possible through the *inclusion* and *assertion* stages into *cooperation*. To do this they have developed exercises and techniques which are effective and which could equally be employed by work or sports teams. However, they are seldom used by team managers for three reasons: because few know about them, because the team members would protest that the psychological exposure involved is not what they joined the team for, and because, not unreasonably, they fear deep responses that they are unequipped to deal with. This is a pity, since team performance could be both accelerated and enhanced by these team-building methods. It will take time for such psychological processes to be seen as less threatening. When it is, it will become more commonplace and its benefits will be more widely acknowledged.

Group exercises

I will illustrate this by giving the examples of two such exercises, which raise or energize the emotions associated with *inclusion* and *assertion* needs. The principle behind activating these emotions is twofold: first, we become experientially aware of their existence; and second, in experiencing, expressing and examining them in the safe environment of a supportive group, we free ourselves from the control that those emotions have over us. In other words, instead of them controlling us subconsciously, we gain conscious control over our emotional state. This is quite the opposite and infinitely more healthy than suppressing emotions.

Extreme cases of the awful effects of suppressed emotions hit our newspapers from time to time in the form of loners who suddenly resort to random violence against a segment of society. Notorious cases that exemplify this are the Unabomer, the Hungerford killings, Jack the Ripper, the Boston Strangler and two dreadful cases early in 1996 when there were fatal shootings of 16 little children and their teacher at a school in Scotland, and 35 day trippers in Tasmania.

The unexpressed inner turmoil that results in such dreadful events resides within all of us in some small measure, often accumulated from early traumas and unresolved emotions. This store of emotions will exert some control over our behaviour of which we are generally barely aware. Unresolved *inclusion* and *assertion* issues account for much of it. It is highly desirable to have the opportunity to explore and release these concealed concerns and emotions in the safe and simulated situation provided by group therapy. The same techniques may be used in a teambuilding context.

Exercises

The following two exercises are examples of the kind of exercises which can be used to address and resolve *inclusion* and *assertion* issues in individuals and teams. They are not party games and should not be used without the presence of an experienced group leader, as the emotional responses evoked by them can be surprisingly strong, and if this occurs these emotions need to be managed safely and constructively. Both exercises are conducted entirely non-verbally, which has the express purpose of heightening the participants' experience of their emotional responses. We tend to talk away our emotions, rather than experience them, which is what is needed here.

Inclusion exercise (sometimes called 'The High School Dance')

The group is divided equally, with each half lined up along opposite walls facing one another. In any order, one person at a time crosses the room and stands in front of the person they wish to be with. That person then indicates whether he or she accepts or rejects the 'invitation to dance'. If the invitation is accepted, the couple go together to a third side of the room. If it is rejected, the inviter has to return to his or her place once more and the process continues until everyone is paired off. There is, however, one complication. If the person you wish to be with has already become paired, you may go to the third side of the room where the pairs now stand and offer yourself in exchange. If accepted, you remain there with your new partner and the 'divorced' partner has to return to his or her original side of the room and start over again.

Until everyone is paired off, powerful emotions about fear of rejection and the need to be accepted hang heavily in the air waiting to be processed. The division of the group at the beginning of the exercise need not be done by sex, of course, but since this sort of pairing is usually done across male–female lines, sexuality issues may be raised by it.

Assertion exercise (known as 'The Dominance Line')

The group is given, say, five minutes to line themselves up along one wall in sequence, with the most dominant person at one end of the line and the most subservient at the other. What ensues is a rare mixture of aggressive, manipulative, sneaky, ruthless, violent, sexist, angry, dejected, humorous, submissive, covert and overt behaviour. Some wait for their opportunity, others feign disinterest, some charge in, others opt out, some never give up, others allow themselves to be trampled on both literally and metaphorically, and occasionally some steadfastly refuse to participate, but eventually they all settle down in their chosen position. Everyone now knows their place and has their space – theoretically of course! In practice a wealth of assertion needs and emotions are exposed by this exercise which can then be addressed within the group.

Review

At the conclusion of each exercise a thorough process review is undertaken. Participants are invited to share their feelings at different moments during the exercise, to comment on their behaviour and to receive feedback from the group. *Inclusion* and *assertion* needs are experienced, expressed and acknowledged and this often leads to insight and resolution. The group is, of course, a microcosm of the world outside and behaviours reflect the way people tend to emote but often repress in their lives. Facing and gaining understanding of those needs in the safety of the group will not only move the group towards *cooperation* but also move the individuals forward in resolving such needs in their lives.

Participants are frequently amazed by the power of their own emotions evoked by these exercises. Most people find that their need for *inclusion* is even greater than their need to *assert* themselves. These are just two of many methods of bringing a group quickly into the *cooperation* stage. A skilful and experienced group therapist may be able to create a *cooperative* group in a matter of hours. Generally it will take longer, say two days of a five-day intensive group.

Group process
In the *assertion* stage the group invariably challenges the leadership of the group and the good leader will welcome this as a natural part of the process, whereas the less experienced leader may wilt, panic or *assert* back with vigorous authoritarianism, which may force obedience but prevents the group from evolving! 'Kill the leader' day usually comes towards the end of the second day of a five-day therapy or business training group. This is not the time for the leader to make an assessment of how well the group is going. Better to wait 24 hours for the 'resurrection' which invariably follows. The more the leader affirms these *assertions* from the group and finds ways to empower group members, the less stressful it will be for everyone. A key way to achieve this is to provide opportunities for the group members to make their own choices and thereby gain ownership of their group.

Among the characteristics displayed by the participants in a *cooperative* therapy group are support, non-competitiveness within the group, concern for the whole, selflessness, compassion, caring and love for the others. In such an environment the participants experience an almost womb-like safety in which they can explore and express their fears and phobias, their anger and anxieties, their pain and passion, and their sorrows and suffering. They can give vent to deep and long-suppressed feelings which needs to be done before they can be free of the burden of their past and move forward.

Indulgence or avoidance

You might be tempted to dismiss such a process as self-indulgent, and it can be, or as unnecessary, which it may be sometimes. Some people consciously and unconsciously seek reasons and ways to avoid self-exploration, for fear of what they might or might not find. Others find it hard to resist the temptation to pursue their own growth, and sooner or later reap the rewards of so doing.

Many people think that they have no unresolved psychological issues to work out, which simply means that they are unaware of what they do have, since all of us have a highly complex psychological history. They also will be unaware of how much some of it holds them back from greater achievement or fulfilment in their lives. They are content with the quality of their lives, only because they have no experience or awareness of what could be.

On the other hand, a growing number of people are becoming aware of blocks to their potential or of a lack of meaning and purpose in their personal and professional lives. With this recognition may come a sense of what could be, and a frustration with what is, but they may have no idea what to do about it. Psychotherapy may have much to offer them.

Subpersonalities

In chapter 2 I mentioned that we are each comprised of a number of subpersonalities which coexist within us, and that each may be maturing at a different rate. This is of particular significance to personal development and psychotherapy. One of the more progressive psychologies is called psychosynthesis, as opposed to psychoanalysis. In lay terms, the first is getting the psyche to pull together and the second is pulling the psyche apart! Psychosynthesis regards subpersonality work as fundamental to the therapeutic process.

Diana Whitmore, my wife, is the chief executive of the London-based Psychosynthesis and Education Trust, an educational charity whose main function is the training of psychosynthesis therapists and people from other professions who seek to broaden or deepen their work with people. In her book *Psychosynthesis Counselling in Action*, she states:

> Subpersonalities are autonomous configurations within the personality as a whole. They are psychological identities, coexisting as a multitude of lives within one person; each with its own specific behaviour pattern, and corresponding self image, body posture, feelings and beliefs. . . Each sub-personality has an exclusive way of responding. We are often quite different when we are with our children to when we are in our workplace. . . When we shift our identifications in this way, it is often in reaction to the demands of the situation. If we are lucky, we are drawn into the sub-personality that is suitable and can act appropriately for the circumstances. More often, however, we are unaware of the expectations from the environment and the demands of our inner world that control us.

From that description, I am sure readers will be able to recognize some of their own different personalities and those of friends and acquaintances. When we experience ambivalence and confusion, it can be seen as a difference of perception or opinion between two or more subpersonalities. Differing body postures and tone and pitch of voice are particularly apparent in some people, as are degrees of assertiveness and reticence displayed in different situations. Each subpersonality has its own needs, values, agenda and priorities. One part of us may be saying that the most important thing in life is to be strong and independent (assertion), while another part wants to belong and be loved (inclusion).

It is not uncommon to find a tyrannical, unsmiling executive at work who at play on the rugby field or in the pub is a laugh a minute. In contrast again, he might be lazy, absent minded and easy going at home with his family, but when he escapes into his passion as a pianist a fourth subpersonality comes to the fore, one that is sensitive and aesthetically refined, 'who marches to the tune of a different drum'. Staying with the musical analogy, some people are like the symphony orchestra before the conductor appears. They are making their own sound for their own purpose. The combination is discordant and chaotic, yet when they work together they make magnificant music.

The psychosynthesis therapist's task is first to have the host of all these little characters recognize and acknowledge their existence, then to accept them. The next stage of the therapy is to have them work out their differences with one another and work through their power struggles. The goal is to bring them together as a harmonious team, all pulling in the same direction for the good of the host.

This is very similar to the process used by a skilful team leader to develop the team and take them through the *inclusion* and *assertion* stages into *cooperation*. Psychosynthesis therapists also use a model of group dynamics which is similar to my three-stage model, but they elaborate the *cooperation* stage into mini-stages or secondary cycles. Dr Roberto Assagioli, a psychoanalyst who trained with Sigmund Freud, founded psychosynthesis in Italy in 1908. Like his colleague Carl Jung, he rejected Freud's limited view of people as being ruled by their lower unconscious and their pathology. He saw them also as being a self on a path of psycho-spiritual evolution. He mapped the evolutionary journey of individuals and groups with the diagram shown in figure 9. Assagioli's model shows that as development occurs behaviour characteristics seem to oscillate back and forth between the two polarities of love and will, which progressively converge. Commitment becomes higher and actions become ever more effective while at the same time the group or individual becomes more caring and *cooperative*, until love and will merge.

This section is not intended to be a justification or a commercial for group therapy but merely to indicate much can be gleaned

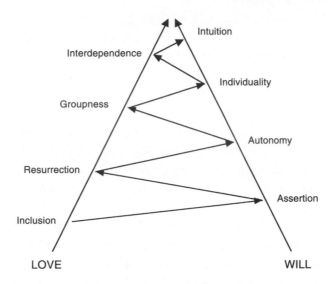

Figure 9: The merging of love and will

from an understanding of how psychotherapy works with groups and individuals. Group therapy can also contribute a lot to our understanding of the three stages of group process or, more broadly, the universality of the evolutionary drive which is contained within each of us.

Spiritual psychologies are very clearly not religions or religious in the sense that they neither require nor impose any kind of faith or belief. There is no doctrine or dogma that has to be learned or adhered to. There is no worship or place of worship. And while the values, attitudes and behaviours of those who have been involved with these psychologies are consistent with the principles of 'Christian living', they are well grounded in psychological principles. I am not in any way suggesting that spiritual psychologies do or should replace religion, but if religion, as we know it, is going to survive the awakening of humankind, it will need to awaken itself and bring a little psychology into its faith, hope and charity.

Religion

Religions are divisive. Of course they are not supposed to be that way, but anyone who claims they are not is simply blind to the reality. Most religions were inspired by God or his messengers, but along the way, sometimes with good intentions, sometimes with bad ones, they became distorted, trivialized and used by godless humans to control the masses, and for personal enrichment or ambition. It is probable that in every religion there are still too many people in high places who are motivated more by the love of power than by the power of love.

This is a harsh judgement and a gloomy picture, but while it is hard to dispute, there is another side too which is less visible and hugely influential. All over the world there are countless humble people, inspired by their religion and guided by its moral code, who have renounced power and material possessions to serve God and humanity in any way they can. They minister to homeless people in inner cities, to those existing in the harsh climates and conditions of poor and poorly managed countries, to those in prison, to the bereaved, to the lonely, the elderly and the terminally sick, and to the innocent victims of natural and man-made disasters in every corner of the world. Their personal and individual embodiment of the love of God is worth more than all the sermons ever preached.

These are two very different and perhaps extreme perspectives of religion today, but we need to take account of both, and all that lies in between, when we look at the impact that religion has on human evolution, and at the evolution of religion itself.

Religions and religious groupings, large and small, follow a similar pattern to all the other groups we have examined so far. Despite the highly *cooperative* espoused ideals and moral values at the heart of every religion, religions have fared no better than most other large social groups in evolutionary terms.

Countless different religious formats cater for every taste and offer a haven or a place to belong. Dependency is encouraged. Once you enter, conformity to group norms, behaviours and beliefs is expected, if not demanded. Individuality and non-conformity are not tolerated. Challenges to church leadership are regarded by the more conservative among the flock as heresy, as the issue of the ordination of women has shown. Most sects and cults too thrive on maintaining a high level of *inclusion* dependency.

While internally every major religion has tended to remain at the level of *inclusion*, opposing religious groups have, for thousands of years, engaged in highly *assertive* behaviour towards each other. 'We are right, and they are wrong.' 'God is with us, and they are servants of the devil.' 'We have the truth, and they are misguided.' 'Our practices will lead you to enlightenment, theirs are false.' These early differences in religious beliefs soon became so hopelessly entwined with socio-economic and political dispute that the primary spiritual purpose and principles became sidelined or manipulated for worldly ends. The tragic primal hostility between Jews and Muslims in the Middle East, Catholics and Protestants in Northern Ireland, Hindus and Sikhs in India, Christians and Muslims in Bosnia-Herzegovina are all ancient and complex mixes of political, economic and religious conflict. The *assertive* behaviour evoked by these differences is deeply ingrained, habitual and mindless. The hostilities are perpetuated for generations as they provide a pretext for violence perpetrated by godless people through *assertion*. Perhaps some do believe they are doing it for God, but God must weep at what is done in his name.

There are of course pockets of *cooperation* both within and between some religious groupings. Inter-faith contact and activities are on the increase. Within the Christian fold there is the ecumenical movement and the World Council of Churches, and locally in the UK the Anglicans and the Catholics have tentatively reached out to each other. Christian-based charitable outreach to the poor, the needy and the oppressed is world-wide and is a significant manifestation of *cooperation* in deed with humanity at large. Other religions, other sects and even individual churches each have their forms of humanitarian *cooperation* often right alongside strong *assertion* and *inclusion* behaviour. But the green shoots of *cooperation* need a lot of nourishment if they are to take hold.

In the previous section I stated that participants in therapy groups which have evolved into the *cooperation* stage display certain qualities. It is interesting to note that these qualities are precisely those which a Christian might describe as Christian values or behaviour. Support, caring, unselfishness, consideration, tolerance of differences, love and the rest. The fact that these qualities emerge from within the group and are not imposed or introduced by the leader suggests that they already reside within people, perhaps just waiting for an opportunity to be expressed. Is this what is meant by the God within? It is highly significant, to me at least, that these are the same qualities that business team members consistently list as the qualities of an ideal work team.

For some, spiritual psychotherapy provides the space and security for the God within to emerge more effectively and authentically than with the church. In religion, there is often a gap between words and actions, as there is in business, but also between the mind and the emotions, between spirituality and psychology and between religious belief and worldly behaviour. Much of what happens in group therapy is non-verbal, in which context the separation between words and actions can not exist. There is a huge difference between saying 'I love you' and being kind to someone; just about the same as the difference between talking about *cooperation* and being *cooperative*.

Religions tend to suggest or demand certain good behaviours and thoughts. Though the intention may be admirable, it completely fails to recognize the path of self-development and the psychological need for *inclusion* (belonging) and *assertion* (self-expression and esteem) to be worked through. It is impossible to coerce people into genuine *cooperative* behaviour if they are not developmentally ready for it, and unnecessary if they are. By the subtle application of threat and repression, people can be forced into adopting apparently cooperative behaviour for a period of time.

This mild or not so mild fire and brimstone approach, which is not uncommon in religious circles, breeds guilt, suppression and resentment, sometimes leading to covert and dangerous *assertive* releases. These *assertions* are liable to manifest themselves as fanatical religious fervour against non-believers, or as psychological self-flagellation, rather than being directed against what is repressing them. This unChristian and very vicious circle is perpetrated by dedicated Christians, and fanatics of other faiths, all over the world. The twin dangers of the psychological ignorance and emotional repression among religions and the religious are great indeed.

Religion is by and large held back somewhere between *inclusion* and *assertion* by a divisive legacy. The values it espouses are those of *cooperation* – those it exhibits are anything but. Authentic moral or *cooperative* values can, and do, emerge from within the human spirit, but that only occurs in a safe, understanding and *cooperative* environment. Religions seem to be incapable of providing this on a wide scale, so they revert to demanding certain moral behaviour which causes more problems than it solves. Without deep psychological reevaluation and the removal of dogma and the lateral and vertical barriers within and between religions, religion will remain incapable of fostering the widespread adoption of moral values, and consequently the harmony (*cooperation*) of the human race. Religion should be leading the awakening of humankind, being a role model of *cooperation*, but it can be argued that a huge culture transformation towards *cooperation* is already beginning in spite of religion, not because of it.

Spirituality

Another kind of spirituality has existed alongside religion for centuries. Sometimes through an unexpected revelation, sometimes through retreat and contemplation, sometimes through art, beauty or music and sometimes through a natural or synthesized hallucinogenic, people have discovered what they may variously describe as God, their soul, themselves, transcendence, inner peace or enlightenment. Such people might be said to have had a spiritual awakening, even if they have no connection past or present to any religion.

Others have been brought up with or in a religion, but later they have 'left the church' and freed themselves from the constraints of the religious dogma that alienated them. They may still practise some of the rituals privately and may even attend a service on occasion, but they retain no attachment to any particular church or even religion.

Many westerners, brought up in the Christian tradition of the external God to be feared and worshipped, feel that something is missing and are attracted to the eastern concept of the God within. They adopt some eastern practices of meditation or yoga and form their own unique blend of the spirituality of the East and the West with allegiance to neither. There is yet another very broad entry point into the spiritual life through healing, through the study of parapsychology, mythology, physics, earth sciences, crop circles and even UFOs. This collection of loosely connected fields used to be called New Age activities until the term became overused and then misused by the tabloid press to describe nomadic malcontents or hippy remnants from the 1960s.

By and large these categories of spiritual people who shun conventional religion have a great deal in common. They are non-dogmatic, they respect and accept each other's different paths, they transcend nationality, cultural and traditional religion, they see the universality of God, they have a vision of a balance between a universal hierarchy without and the Self or the God within which is remarkably consistent, their spirituality is rooted in their experience rather than in theological theory and their nature is *cooperative*. While there are exceptions on both sides, my experience of these kind of people is that they embrace the loving essence of religion with greater comfort than those who fit the conventional criteria of being religious. They show the way to a *cooperative* world much more convincingly.

13
Where Are We Going?

It is not my intention here to give a history lesson. That has been done many times and much more comprehensively by people far better equipped than I. It is, however, necessary to draw a sketch map of the influences and changes in thinking that have taken place in the past couple of millennia to enable me to position the *assertion* stage, in which we currently are, both in time and in terms of classical analysis.

The development of western civilization is conventionally described as a series of major epochs, characterized by key ideas and values as expressed through the church, art, architecture and politics of the time. If we take a quick journey though this we can see the emergence of the ideas and values which shape our modern world and may shine some light on where we go from here.

The earlier we begin our journey, the greater was the influence of religion on our social development and on our thinking. Central to Judaism were the concepts of only one God for all and of the possibility of salvation. This introduced the idea of life being purposeful leading towards a meaningful end. Human endeavour was valued.

Early Christianity built on these ideas and values. There was in fact an eruption of consciousness, compassion, charity, hope and beauty associated with God. The monastic life of selfless detachment developed, and it was due to the monasteries that the values of Christianity were kept alive during the Dark Ages, AD 700 to 1000, when barbarian invasions occurred all over Europe.

Light returned in the Middle Ages, from the year 1000 to 1400, and this constitutes the *inclusion* stage of our current cultural cycle. Relative survival and security needs were met, but life was tough and people's hopes lay in the beyond. God was at the centre of life. People were dependent on God and his churchly representatives, to whose wishes they conformed without question or even much thought. It was the time of pilgrimages and crusades. Gothic architecture and technology enabled the buildings to be constructed higher 'to reach God' and with thinner walls containing windows, particularly stained glass, 'to bring in more light'. Stimulation and communication for a largely illiterate population were visual and aural. Beauty itself and beautiful things were seen to lead to God. The concept of valuing the feminine, of courtly or romantic love, brought gracious refinement and had a civilizing impact. Religious expression was characterized by the mystical and the irrational.

The Renaissance which followed began as the rebirth of the lost tradition of the past, of Plato and Aristotle. It emphasized the dignity of man at the centre of his own experience. It was of course the beginning of our present *assertion* stage. It brought individuality and perspective into art and life. The invention of printing enabled people to read and decide for themselves, and to question authority. (It is hard to imagine the Bible as the first industrial commodity!) The word itself gave people power. The focus began to shift from Heaven to Earth. The characteristics of *assertion* were all present, though in relatively mild form at first. It was a self-confident time during which we pushed our boundaries physically, we circumnavigated the globe and logical thought triumphed over feeling. It was the age of discovery in which the world began to lose its mystery and was rationalized on to maps.

The Reformation was a time of challenge to authority politically and socially, prefiguring the greater changes to come in the 19th century. Martin Luther nailed his Theses to the door of the church at Wittenburg in 1517 in a defiant challenge to the authority of Rome. The Catholic Church mounted a counter reformation in an attempt to turn back to the values of the past and seduce people back to their church. It was the time of overly elaborate church architecture, especially apparent in Austria, and of decorative art and music known as the Baroque period. Under the guise of defending the Catholic Church the Spanish expressed their imperial and inquisitorial excesses. However, the centralized power and authority of the Church of Rome and of all churches continued to be devolved and to decline.

The so-called Age of Enlightenment followed, with the elevation of reason and the beginning of science as we know it. There was a more definitive break with the authority of the church and a growing confidence that man could work out the answers for himself. Increasingly science replaced theology as the key to understanding, and mathematics and economics replaced myths and morals. Optimism in man's ability to shape his world and a belief in the future and in progress replaced previous pessimism. The only obstacles to progress were seen as the intolerance, ignorance and parochialism of the past. A critical attitude developed in which nothing was sacred.

The Romantic period, from 1770 to 1830, was a reaction against overemphasis on rational thought and outer organization. Value was attached to feelings, instinct and intuition, often without regard to personal cost. History and the past were seen as important. The journey for self-fulfilment and the search of the soul were seen as more relevant than the surface of life. It was a poetic world of wonder, fantasy and the demonic, but the ultimate union was death. However, the French Revolution of 1793 and the exploits of Napoleon put reason on a pedestal.

Before 1865, two-thirds of the population of Britain lived in communities of 10,000 or less, but the advent of railways and the Industrial Revolution lead to demographic change and an urban explosion. Equality, freedom and democracy were further debated and valued. The end of the 19th century saw the emergence of social and political movements; workers began to *assert* their previously non-existent rights; trade unions were formed leading to the founding of the Labour Party. The concept of the nation-state supplanted both the sacred community and the monarchical empire. The resultant international competition was to lead eventually to the First World War.

Modernism is the artistic, intellectual and musical expression of the modernization which occurred from the beginning of 20th century as capitalism, industrialization and democracy interacted with each other. It both celebrated and was critical of the break with tradition. A big gap arose between science and religion. Freud and others questioned rationality and progress, but discoveries in science, mass communication, the advent of the car and the aeroplane heralded a culture of innovation and change. Ease of travel expanded the capitalist market. The belief was that science would lead us to utopia.

Postmodernism is a body of thought which develops the more pessimistic strands of modernism. Linguistic philosophy suggested that the word is all there is, but we become trapped by the word which defines, limits and eventually deceives us. Postmodernism incorporates the notion of the post-industrial society. It suggests that there has been a key change in economic political and cultural life since the beginning of the 1970s, characterized by fragmentation, ephemerality, discontinuity and a sense of the chaotic. There are no universal truths. Progress and rationality lead nowhere. All utopias end in repression. How politicians look has become more important than how they act in the new media-saturated world. Corporate identities are manipulated by presentation and capital.

In this unpredictable period, there is no agreed standard of values. Pessimism has been increased by the recognition of the inevitability of two devastating world wars in which 80 million people died, by the symbolic horror of Hiroshima, and by the naked napalmed children in Vietnam, which seemed to change nothing. The massive build-up of appalling weaponry world-wide, the spread of terrorism leading to the fear of nuclear terrorism, and environmental degradation continue and are further evidence, if we need it, of hopelessness – and of *assertion* gone mad.

Plurality has given a voice to many but has led to more insecurity and uncertainty. The drug culture, sexual abuse, violence in schools and in the soccer stands, and endemic unemployment threaten our children. The speed and increased volume of information have caused overload and fragmentation. Economies are supersensitive and fragile. The intensity of the present has produced a loss of self, of the past and of a future. This is the prevailing critical mood of our postmodern age – a fear for the future and a loss of faith in the human project. And this is about where the classical thinking stands today.

I challenge this popular nihilism. In my opinion there *is* a future, and this period of confusion and pessimism can equally be seen as the swan song, the death throes of the age of *assertion*. There may be some years in which we have to ride the storm before the stabilizing effect of *cooperation* is felt. On the other hand it may come far faster than we expect, for change is now exponential.

Kinsman's future

In 1990 business consultant Francis Kinsman wrote a fascinating book entitled *Millennium 2000: Towards Tomorrow's Society*. It is an analysis of our business culture and the wider culture of which business is a part. It interprets where we have come from and speculates on where we are going. He shares with me the belief in the relevance of Maslow's developmental model to society as a whole and he draws extensively on the findings of a study prepared by Taylor Nelson Monitor during 1985 for the National Economic Development Office. This refers to three stages of human development which equate very closely to our three-stage model. Kinsman identifies 29 per cent of the British population as those derived from the agricultural era, whom he describes as sustenance driven or in our terms driven by *inclusion* needs. He says that 35 per cent of the population are products of the industrial era, whom he describes as outer directed or we might say *assertive*. The remaining 36 per cent from the post-industrial era he calls inner directed and I call *cooperative*. His percentages are very optimistic using my definitions, but he puts the boundaries in a different place because he uses a different set of criteria, characteristics which enable him to place people within seven social value groups. Table 5 shows the social value groups, the characteristics associated with each, the percentages in each category in 1987 and how they aggregate into the three main categories.

Francis Kinsman's highly entertaining book provides fascinating insights and observations about our society and many anecdotes to support his interpretation of how our culture is evolving. His commentary is as relevant today as it was in 1990. Unfortunately the book is now out of print, but those who wish to explore these concepts in more depth may still obtain copies direct from the author (details in the appendix). I highly recommend it.

Kinsman postulated three possible futures by extrapolation of current trends. With his permission I reproduce extracts from them here,

Table 5: The social value groups

Social value group	Characteristics	% 1987	Aggregation into major categories
Self-explorers	Ethical, tolerant, open, understanding, introspective, non-materialistic and individualistic	15	Inner directed – 36%
Social resistors	Altruistic, concerned with social views and supporters of standards but also doctrinaire, intolerant and moralistic	14	
Experimentalists	Unconventional, technological, creative, self-confident, physically fit, risk oriented, self-indulgent	11	
Conspicuous consumers	Acquisitive, competitive, assertive, conscious of appearances, authoritarian and materialistic	22	Outer directed – 35%
Belongers	Conservative, pragmatic, traditionalist, conventional, self-sacrificing, tribal and pedantic	17	
Survivors	Sustenance driven, class conscious, community minded, traditionalist, cheerful, awkward if treated badly but quietly hard working if treated well	15	Sustenance driven – 29%
Aimless	Either old, lonely, purposeless and disinterested; or young, hostile, anti-authoritarian and frequently violent	16	

including his speculative but illustrative newspaper headlines of the day.

The retrenchment scenario

The bear market continues its progress of deep downturns interspersed with shallow upturns. This will eventuate into an American-led or Japan-led recession which will ultimately be so severe that even in the short term it leads to a sickening collapse in the other industrialised countries of the west and almost more importantly, to an even steeper slump in commodity prices.

Consumer Riots in Oxford Street – 7 Shot by Security Guards

Six women and an elderly man, wounds this afternoon, after the most serious of the current wave of consumer riots brought on by acute shortages of essential goods. Caveat Emptor, members of the consumer movement, were hospitalised with gunshot

This has its most damaging effect on the Third World producer countries that rely on them for the servicing of their colossal overhang of international debt. In the past their defaults or potential defaults have been countered by what is politely termed 'rescheduling'. This process entails the rolling up of interest which is added to the capital sums outstanding, and combined with the lending of additional money in order to afford the new and larger payments. When you boil this down, it has amounted to a hope that continued inflation would mean that neither banks nor governments would have to write off these debts. With the old loans being paid in new money, equal in nominal terms but considerably less in real terms, the emperor's clothes might still be thought to keep him sufficiently decent.

However, this concept has always relied on the ability and willingness of lender governments, lender banks and global lenders of last resort like the World Bank and the International Monetary Fund

Sunday Porn from Space – Satellite TV's Naughty New Series

Goggle TV, the ninth satellite company to hit the airwaves, plans a regular programme of explicit sex during Sunday prime-time. 'We are fulfilling a genuine need for fun and excitement,' claimed Chief Goggle's Executive Adrian Lustfinger aboard his luxury yacht, the Mafiavelli.

to play along with the fabrication. But if suddenly they themselves are subjected to a squeeze so that they need the money back – at the same time as the ultimate provider, the United States, is bust both internally and externally – we are all in considerable trouble.

The international currency crash that could follow the recognition of this reality would leave 1929 et seq. looking like a parachute drop as compared to a free-fall. It would usher in a period of intense depression during which greedy outer directed values would be at a serious discount and where the call would be for revenge against all those who had contributed to this disaster or might conceivably have benefited from it. Sustenance driven values would pertain, for a while at any rate, and the price of turnips would be a more significant news item than the level of the Share Index.

In this scenario, there is a greater reliance on large organisations, both public and private, which project an image of stability and security. But, given the overwhelming sense of economic drabness and panic, the collectivist approach is favoured, particularly in the shape of multinational or state-owned nationalised enterprises.

Eleven Ways of Cooking Turnips
The humble root, palate. Turnips à la when treated with mode d'Orléans are imagination can be by no means, as has resource, orchestrated to been rumoured, re- tempt even the Joan's final re- most demanding venge against the English.

These conditions could become too acute for any of the traditional political parties to provide effective leadership, so an authoritarian, either extreme left or right wing, regime might well result. A new government of this sort could well start by instituting measures to protect the public from the violence of the young unemployed. As these measures intensify, the regime becomes more despotic and adopts an increasingly nationalistic and protectionist posture.

As regards work and employment, in some sectors there would be an increase in trade union influence and muscle, with a strong token belief in the 'right to work' which it is up to society or the state to fulfil. But, in its turn, management is bureaucratic, hierarchical, authoritarian and rigid. Unemployment is widespread and scores of applicants fight for every job. Those who have conserved their resources by judicious manipulation are still at the mercy of the vast army of have-nots who unrestrainedly harass them, steal from them, defraud them and even threaten them with bodily violence.

Petrol Coupon Lorry Hijack
An armed securi- van, carrying two months supply of petrol coupons to Aberdeen, was held up at gunpoint yes- terday on the hard should of the M1 near Rugby. The five members of the gang got away with a haul having an estimated black-market value of £1.75 million.

The assertive materialism scenario

An aggressively materialistic stance is the flavour of the month here, as long as the economic clouds somehow roll by and the world in general and Britain in particular turn out to be on the threshold of a prolonged period of growth, underpinned by the view that science and technology have finally delivered all the answers.

The thrust is towards the full rich life, with an emphasis on living for today and escaping from any whisper of an unpleasant reality of social and global problems. People group together to beat any threat of an economic crisis by the old-fashioned means of grind, efficiency and productivity.

They believe that economic growth will solve all problems, yet some also use work as a means of avoiding the personal and societal problems they cannot face. The key words are prestige, status, power and success. Large, successful multinational organisations and strong central governments are applauded for their efforts to develop the economy. Duty is accepted as a norm; people ache to be respected, to be successful and (to appear to be) well off.

CBI Chief Slams Green Wallies

Industrial leader Sir Jasper Thunderblast used the CBI conference platform to mount a blistering attack on 'limp environmentalists' who are trying to hold back progress. 'People want jobs; people want money; people want success. The natterjack toad and the lesser spotted woodpecker come pretty low down on their list of priorities.'

Organisations grow to even greater size, sometimes organically but more often by merger, until a small number of them dominate the world economy. The outer directeds who call the shots are organisation men who seek the status and rewards which these large prestigious enterprises can provide. They tend to favour mammoth, privately-owned economic enterprises, but many also have a burning wish to start their own businesses.

Identity Card Scheme Mooted

Plans for a National Identity Card system are to be set out in a Green Paper due for publication next month. The recent inner city crime wave has alarmed ministers, who are also under pressure from Brussels to bring British practice into line with her European partners. Scotland Yard's Chief Commissioner Bernard Lash welcomed the news. 'Only those who have something to hide have anything to fear', he said.

However for most of them the motivation is to make money and to show they have made it, unlike the inner directed entrepreneur whose motivation is to create something valuable and fulfil a personal vision.

Stress – the Price to Be Paid

Leading cardiologists are concerned about the ever-growing numbers of heart attack victims in our competitive society. Luxury lifestyles, long hours and high performance demands are taking their toll of those at the top. But increasingly the economic explosion is detonating people up and down the whole scale.

Within organisations the marketing, sales and financial functions become even more influential. There is a close relationship between contribution and responsibility on the one hand and salary on the other, so that people are prepared to work exceptionally hard to enhance their own qualifications in order to get ahead. Unemployment has now been markedly reduced by the high level of economic activity, but not for those with the wrong skills or who live in the wrong geographical location.

The caring autonomy scenario

The economic emphasis is on 'good growth' and 'sustainable development', a steady improvement in the quality of life rather than a hectic boom that carries with it the seeds of a subsequent bust.

It is a more caring world with a safety net for those who are genuinely deprived, but at the same time there is a strong reaction against any collective organisation of welfare, since individual freedom and individual responsibility are so highly valued. Implicit within this responsibility, however, is the demand that people involve themselves with others who are less fortunate, and help to bring them to their own fulfilment.

In the political arena there are two new movements. The old polarisation is giving way to consensus and compromise among the small cells and local networks that are springing up all over the place; secondly, the process of government is moving from top down to bottom up.

There is a growing emphasis on the understanding of inter-personal processes, compromise, tolerance and empathy. In the planning sphere citizens are constructing new, small, interrelated institutions for themselves. There is a great sense of urgency for people to become involved in the life of their own neighbourhood and community; single issue groups proliferate. There is pressure for more decisions to be taken at local level rather than in Whitehall and indeed for central government's role to diminish to that of an overall coordinator and representative in global matters.

The Dole – a State Salary

The unemployed are beginning to treat their benefit as something they can pass on to the community as a whole. BURN, the British Unemployment Resource Network, cites the case of painter and decorator, Scott Oldcastle, 29, who having been made redundant, has now set up a free service for old-age pensioners in his native Sheffield.

The Knowledge Industry – Britain's Powerbase

As manufacturing industry and technology are increasingly being transferred to developing countries like Taiwan, Mexico and Nigeria, the export of knowledge, training and education is being recognised as the key to Britain's steady progress.

The working society has become highly complex with new forms of organisational structure, reflecting the predisposition of inner directeds towards small-scale institutions and activities in which they can do things their own way. Consultancies, open networks and overlapping cells flourish rather than hierarchies and bureaucracies. Large organisations show a tendency to split down into federalised and project-based units, human factors in business are emphasised and interrelatedness, openness and trust are demanded of managements.

Charity Begins at Home

Last year, Britain's charities collected a record £3 billion in donations from the public, over 10% more than ever before. The annual report of the Charity Commissioners emphasises the trend towards personal commitment in charitable concern. 'Just signing a cheque is no longer enough,' says the report's introduction, 'people now want to get involved as well.'

Unemployment is less of a stigma among the majority and people are thus not so susceptible to feelings of rejection and better able to find or create new innovative opportunities for themselves.

Kinsman is careful to avoid suggesting a particular date for these scenarios, but table 6 gives an indication of his time scale, and suggests how the composition of social groupings might change.

Table 6: Percentages of social groupings under three alternative scenarios

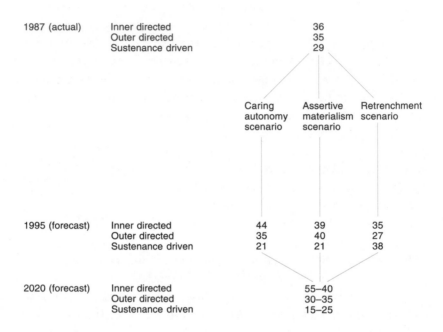

1987 (actual)	Inner directed	36
	Outer directed	35
	Sustenance driven	29

		Caring autonomy scenario	Assertive materialism scenario	Retrenchment scenario
1995 (forecast)	Inner directed	44	39	35
	Outer directed	35	40	27
	Sustenance driven	21	21	38
2020 (forecast)	Inner directed		55–40	
	Outer directed		30–35	
	Sustenance driven		15–25	

Synthesis, which took over the work of Taylor Nelson, produced figures in 1994 which show an evolutionary regression rather worse than the retrenchment scenario forecast in the original research. This is explained in part by refinements to the original model, but mainly by the fact that social resisters have dropped from the inner directed category right down to the sustenance driven category. The reason for this is that this previously progressive segment of society has aged, and has at the same time been hit by the recession, both factors causing them to regress into self-protectiveness. I will refrain from political comment! Belongers are now split half and half between being sustenance driven and outer directed, so the new figures which should be seen in conjunction with those in table 6 are as follows:

Self-explorers	11%	Inner directed
Experimentalists	10%	21%
Conspicuous consumers	18%	Outer directed
Belongers (half)	10%	28%
Belongers (half)	10%	
Social resisters	12%	Sustenance driven
Survivors	23%	51%
Aimless	6%	

These figures appear to contradict the evolutionary movement towards *cooperation*; however, evolutionary time scales are vast, and this is no more than a hiccup in the inevitable. Kinsman's future persuasively challenges the pessimism of postmodernism. Other challenges are on the horizon too, from unexpected quarters.

14
Science, Technology and Beyond

Realism has tempered the expectation that science will lead us to utopia. Research rushes on in too many areas to discuss here, but we will take a brief look at chaos. Likewise it is hard to imagine, let alone predict, what new technology and chips will soon be on the menu and which dish might give us indigestion. What are the social implications of information technology providing everyone with everything they wish to know and more? Not only can we overload the mind in a nanosecond, we can overload the senses too and cause a fuse to blow. Virtual reality offers sensational prospects for us and our inner world. At the same time information technology has so shrunk the globe that as more of the universe comes into view, we speculate on what or who is out there.

From chaos to *cooperation*

Anyone with a passing interest in science is likely to have heard of the concept of chaos or catastrophe theory. They are also likely to find the terms somewhat alarming but to have very little idea as to what they mean. Along with general systems theory, cybernetics and others, they form what is collectively known as the sciences of complexity. What they have in common is the notion that apparently chaotic systems from minute molecules to grand social structures are subject to unpredictable leaps of self-organization into greater complexity at a higher level of organization.

Statements like that never mean much to me without an

accompanying mental image. A commonly used illustration of self-organization at work occurs when water is sloshing about in a sink at the time the waste plug is pulled. For a while the water appears to behave randomly and then, quite suddenly and for no apparent reason, a swirl and a funnel appears and the water settles into a coherent system as the water leaves the sink 'in a highly organized way'.

It is not my intention to be, nor am I capable of being, overly scientific, but the social transformation that we are currently undergoing, in our model the shift from *assertion* to *cooperation*, seems to fit the chaos model. That is perhaps not so surprising, since complexity theorists suggest that these principles apply to all systems regardless of their size or the nature of their components.

It is not hard to see that our western *assertive* society is experiencing a fair degree of chaos. We have grown to accept a degree of random social disruption and violence that would have alarmed anyone ten years ago. The economic indicators that governments, economists and business leaders used to rely on are no longer reliable. Institutions, never perfect, are now seen to have cracks in their fabric and perhaps in their foundations. No one seems to be able to respond. The glue that held together our capitalist society, competitiveness and *assertiveness*, may be coming unstuck.

There is no question also that *cooperation* is a more complex but higher level of organization than our present chaotic state. It promises another period of stability, even if that stability is one of continuous and dynamic evolution. When exactly the breakthrough will occur, what will trigger it and how much more of a breakdown will have to occur first is anyone's guess. Of course in practice, transformational leaps are already occurring in many of our social subsystems. We just do not seem to be able to control them the way assertive people like to. They are self-organizing.

A small interference in one part of the system can have a quite unpredictable impact on another, apparently disconnected part. Of course, none of it is disconnected. Plenty of illustrations of this are to be found as we degrade one part of our environmental system which results in an extinction in another part, or an excess in a third. Systems seem to have a self-organizing will of their own. We can unwittingly alter the course of a system, and we are always a part of an ever bigger system. It is up to us to choose if we go with the flow or try to swim against the tide. The tide is a highly complex, exquisitely ordered system, and riding the surf from chaos to *cooperation* might be a real thrill.

Virtual reality

On 8 January 1908, a Czechoslovakian scientist, Nikolae Tesla, announced that he knew how to provide us with pictures in our homes of events occurring simultaneously in other parts of the world. He was ridiculed and written off. In 1932 Scotsman Logie Baird demonstrated television for the first time. By 1960, 10 million households had TV, by 1990 this had risen to 22 million households, and these contained 35 million TV sets. Today there are as many simultaneous events or simulated events as you could wish for. Home computers are fast becoming as prolific and interactive CD-ROM gives us another dimension. Computer games are becoming ever more realistic. The Internet can take us anywhere for anything. Now on the horizon is another piece of technology which threatens to have an even bigger impact than any of these when it invades our homes. The time from invention to invasion has shrunk tenfold. Before this book is out of print, you will be spending a part of each day in virtual reality.

Television allows us to switch channels, but virtual reality allows us to switch our experience. Television allows us to participate vicariously in sport, visually and audially; virtual reality will allow us to experience sport fully in our front room. Television can give us repeats, close-ups and slow motion; virtual reality will be able to give us all that and more – things in fact that reality can not give us. Virtual reality will give us options of shape, size, colour, sound and feel that reality itself can not do. Virtual reality is better than reality. That logic is inescapable and scary.

Its potential for misuse, abuse and addiction is so obvious and so great that ethical and legal arguments will ensue. Televisual sex and online porn are already less risky healthwise and according to aficionados, more regularly satisfying, cheaper and far less embarrassing or demanding than a date; and besides, 'you can always switch to someone else or switch them off'. The mind boggles at the potential for virtual sex, to which a branch of science called dildonics is devoted.

Consciousness-altering, sensory-enhancing and mind-bending drugs may provide awesome images that defy verbal description, enable users to see humour in every nuance of their surroundings or cause a sudden free fall into darkness, despair, terror or paranoia. We have precious little choice over which we get other than by creating the right environment for the hoped-for experience. That, however, is no guarantee, because the immediate mental state, psychological history and biochemical interactions of the user seem to be the determining factors, all of which are largely outside our control. Virtual mind manipulation, on the other hand, is entirely controllable and infinitely variable.

The current version of virtual reality approaches the mind via the senses through the use of goggles, gloves and simulators. The technological advance that makes all this equipment redundant and opens up far more possibilities is that we now know how to stimulate the centres in the brain that control experience directly. It will be possible in another decade or so for us to create any multisensory experience we wish to have at the push of a button. It will be better than the real thing because it is instant, alterable at will, safe, cheap and requires no props or other people.

Regulation, however, will not be so easy. Technological creativity is unstoppable. If it can be done it will be, and to hell with the consequences. That is how all weapons of mass destruction, from the Gatling gun to the hydrogen bomb, came into being. Werner von Braun created the Second World War missile the V2 which terrorized London, but he did not want to kill people: his passion was rocketry and war provided the opportunity for him to exercise it. After the war the Americans enabled him to continue pursuing his passion which before long took man to the moon. Great advances in science and technology have no conscience; people may have. Genetic manipulation is the subject of much heated ethical debate by the powers that be, while the powers that invent are heads down in their laboratories from dawn till dusk salivating over their possibilities. So it is with virtuality.

In the same way that Francis Kinsman postulated three future scenarios, virtual reality opens up three rather more wild speculative futures, one evolutionary, one transformational and one terminal. The journey of each is virtually the same, but the outcome is very different. I illustrate them here not because I think that one or the other will occur as I describe it, but to make us think about the consequences of not managing our forthcoming technological leaps with foresight and <u>responsibility</u>. It will be up to us to choose our own reality.

Evolution

Assertion is all about quantity and *cooperation* is all about quality. Whether one starts the clock at the beginning of modern science or at the beginning of the Industrial Revolution, the period in between has been dominated by the demand to produce more, bigger, faster and for less. For many decades better has become less and less important, and if it is mentioned it is more lip service than reality. The quality of household goods today from furniture to table knives is worse than it was by any criteria, save that of manufacturing expediency and profit potential, than it was a hundred years ago. The same is true of the quality of children's art or handwriting, dressmaking and household handicrafts. Even cars of 60 or more years ago were beautifully made compared to the technological marvels we rush around in now which rot and rust on demand after the designated lifespan has expired. The lifespan is one of carefully calculated built-in obsolescence, combined with a life that is reliable enough to delude us into thinking that the car is well built.

Quality can refer to how well we make something, how well that something does its job, how long it is able to do that job for or how useful that job is. The demands of capitalism and economic growth have changed the way we think even about what is good, but hasn't it gone too far? The widespread hankering after things that are old and classic in every field has frequently taken even the speculators by surprise. When I was a professional racing driver in the 1960s, last year's racing car was not worth the metal it was made of. We scrapped cars at the end of a racing season, cars like Shelby Cobras and Ford GT 40s, which by 1988 would have been worth up to a million pounds a piece. What do people want with these old things? The quality, and a sprinkling of nostalgia.

The question of quality that is most neglected today is the usefulness of the task. Perhaps that is because so much has been subsumed to the profit motive that a product is assumed to be useful if it is profitable and no other questions matter. However, if we are in *cooperative* mode the usefulness of the job does matter. For whom is it useful? Is that fair? What fairer job could we do with the same resources? Is it needed or just wanted? Does the job create winners here, but losers there? What are the by-products and side-effects of doing the job?

If we had rigorously sought answers to these questions applied to nuclear fission, cars, television, the microprocessor and many other of the technological advances of this century, the world we live in today might have been a better place. We did not because technology made a sudden leap way ahead of the qualitative development of our consciousness that was essential for the responsible management of the application of this technology. Has our consciousness caught up? No. We must ask these questions of virtual reality. We must find qualitatively better applications for it than profit and kicks. Of course that is already happening, such as in the fields of medicine, and in skills training, flight simulators for training pilots have been around for years. If we were to use virtual reality for *cooperative* purposes rather than *assertive* ones, it could become an aid to human evolution. If we predominantly go the other way, it may develop into a new Skid Row. We could engage in a series of virtual wars and all end up virtually dead.

Human beings are, however, remarkably resilient, and evolution is a very powerful force working away behind the scenes. I am optimistic that sooner or later we will bring quality back into the equation as we approach the stage or age of *cooperation*. If it is sooner, this great new technological innovation called virtual reality may help us create a better reality for all.

Extinction

Many animals can see better than human beings, and many can hear better. Many birds can sing more beautifully, and we don't smell too good either! However, we have made television and telescopes to help us see the farthest galaxies and microscopes to see other specks of dust, microphones that can pick up the smallest sound, telephones to hear and talk to our friends the other side of the world and musical instruments of all kind. We have even invented an electronic nose with which to test the finest wines and perfumes.

Many animals can run faster than human beings, we are not that good at jumping, we are clumsy in the water and we cannot fly at all. We have no sharp teeth to bite our enemies or claws to fight them with, and we don't pack the kick of a mule. However, we have invented cars, trains, skis, dirt bikes and mountain bikes which can outstrip the fleetest animal on its own ground. We have poles to vault with, bungees to jump with, balloons and helicopters to keep us up for longer, and parachutes and hang gliders to let us down gently. We have built boats of all sizes from surfboards to ocean liners, and submarines and scuba equipment to get us down under. We have built flying machines that fly faster than sound, and we have flown to the moon and back. We have equipped ourselves with knives, handguns and more sophisticated weapons with which we can threaten, dominate or vaporize any place or living thing on earth.

We ourselves do not do anything particularly well, but we do have the unique ability to invent complex tools to enable us to do literally anything we are capable of imagining. And now with virtual reality we can experience literally anything we can imagine without even having to do it.

As we have developed and become accustomed to using these tools, we increasingly rely on them to make up for our physical limitations, and we get lazy. We don't even have to be particularly physically fit now, as our tools become more and more comfortable and user friendly. We can fly or drive or sail the oceans in armchair comfort with instruments to guide us. We hardly have to do anything. We hardly have to think. By the use of interconnected technologies, a ruthless tyrant can 'take out' an enemy on another continent without leaving the comfort of his drawing room. We have learned how to assemble these technologies in customized combinations to do it all for us at the touch of a button. We do not even have to touch the button now, for a thought can set the machinery in motion. Soon we won't even give it a thought.

Why do we need a body at all? With which to experience all the marvellous things we can do, perhaps. However, doing them from an armchair has taken the sensation out of them. So we invented virtual reality to give us the thrill back by stimulating our bodily senses, with no real risk to ourselves. Now we find that we can stimulate the brain directly and we do not even need our senses – or our body. Just a wired-up brain will do. The inevitable conclusion of the journey of man the toolmaker is that physical existence becomes redundant. So where does that leave us, or what is left of us?

That all sounds like pretty bad news, but is it? Darwin gave us the survival of the fittest, and each species naturally selected those characteristics which ensured its survival. Our biology did not look too good, but our biography got us the job of top species because we had the skill of toolmaking. Toolmaking enabled us to adapt to our environment, any environment, and to ward off danger, any danger. Could it be that toolmaking enables us to take the next giant leap in evolution? Thanks to the misuse of our tools, our planet is being seriously degraded; but if we don't need a body, do we need a planet?

The majority of people today believe that we are not alone in the universe. They believe that out there somewhere are other intelligent life forms, probably some of them billions of years in evolutionary advance of us. Do you really suppose that they are still clumping around in clumsy physical bodies like ours? Would they not have learned how to dispense with their bodies, and therefore transcend time and space? They would not need to visit us in physical form; indeed they could not, for physical space travel will always be just too slow to get anywhere far. Aside from the odd alleged physical alien, most of our visitors have been on a very much more ethereal plane. We have called them angels, archangels and even God, and they have been long on ethics and love and kindly guidance, but short on hardware and demands. Might they simply be beings who have evolved beyond the need for physical bodies and a planet on which to set them down?

Transformation

There is a kind of Orwellian scenario in the potential of virtual reality. Whether we have tried is questionable, but we have not succeeded in improving the lot of the poor in our world. Infant mortality remains high; the poor tend to inhabit areas that are subject to drought or flooding, with dreadful consequences; food is scarce, healthcare is minimal and water is polluted – in other words, their basic **needs** are not met.

However, there are millions, perhaps billions more whose basic needs are met but their quality of life is hardly worth living for. They live lives of quiet desperation, working in repetitive jobs with little prospect of improvement. They bring home enough pay to feed the family, pay the mortgage and take an annual holiday in Spain. They buy a lottery ticket each week, go to the football match and the pub on a Saturday and watch soaps on television the rest of the week. The kids have few prospects and no hope. Boredom and frustration drive them to petty crime, drugs or senseless acts of violence and vandalism, and sooner or later they are back to follow in their parents' dragging footsteps. The only thing that makes the predicament tolerable for these families is the belief that it has always been that way, that it probably always will be and it is that way for most of their friends, so they acquiesce, grumble a bit and play the game.

That is a caricature, but I suspect we can all recognize a bit of ourselves in that scenario. Is that really what life is supposed to be like? Is life supposed to be any particular way?

Perhaps we unconsciously chose it the way it is. We did not have the courage to break the mould. However, along comes a salesperson with a device which we can attach to our minds and transform our experience regardless of the reality. At a touch of a button it can sweep us on to the highest mountain or to the bottom of the ocean. We can have experiences which previously were exclusively available only to the very brave, skilful, rich or famous. It is better than drugs, better than sex and better than a pint of beer. Is this the way out of it all? So what if it is vegetative and mentally addictive. Virtual reality, like so many high-tech toys, may start as an indulgence for the rich and end up as the panacea for the poor – and everyone in between. Is this the future? Or is this the end?

When human beings have all been made redundant and technology does all the work, we will need virtual reality to escape the boredom and squalor of our polluted planet. We can just plug in, turn on and be transported into an infinitely more attractive virtual reality, while we, along with other forms of life on earth, just quietly lay down to die.

Higher intelligence

If there is any basis for belief in the presence of higher intelligence in the universe, regardless of what form it might take, it has profound implications for our future. By higher intelligence I mean extra-terrestrial intelligence, life forms of some sort with intelligence more sophisticated and evolved than our own. These minds may or may not be located in a physical body, which may or may not be based on other physical planets in other solar systems. If we believe in the existence of God and an angelic hierarchy, they could also be described as extra-terrestrial intelligence. Some UFO cultists see the only hope of salvation being provided by aliens visiting us from or transporting us to other worlds.

In August 1996 US President Clinton, excited by the prospect of microscopic life on Mars, relit the Space Agency fuse. However, it should not be forgotten that the search for extra-terrestrial intelligence (SETI) is already a serious business. In 1992 NASA invested a great deal of effort, money and new technology in searching the stars, or rather their planets, for radio signals which might indicate the presence of intelligent life forms. On a British TV programme entitled *ET, Please Phone Earth*, several eminent professors involved with the project expressed little doubt that such life exists and were anxious for Earth to keep listening for signs of it.

However, they were not all in agreement about the wisdom of us Earthlings revealing our presence to the wider universe. As one luminary pointed out, we all know what we humans did to societies that we deemed to be more primitive when we discovered them, so what might more advanced life forms do to us? That fear is based on the contradictory assumption that these 'advanced' beings would be as aggressive, thoughtless, uncompassionate and primitive as human beings!

It is too late now anyway, for we have been sending out radio messages for many decades, the first of which have already sped past neighbouring solar systems. But the bizarre nature of the more powerful signals that follow those first dots and dashes, from soap operas to evangelical preachers, might cause an alien to wonder whether intelligent life does exist on Earth after all! When Mahatma Gandhi was asked what he thought about western civilization, he said 'it would be a good idea'. Such might be the view of Earth from afar...

The threat posed to us by travellers from other worlds which was fostered by early science fiction books, Orson Welles's famous broadcast and many films is today reinforced by strange stories of cattle mutilations and UFO abductions. However, more recently, perhaps initiated by Gene Roddenberry's *Star Trek*, there have been several cinematic attempts to present extra-terrestrial life as benign, although the 1996 blockbuster *Independence Day* reversed the trend with firestorming intelligent octopi.

Years ago physicist John Wheeler postulated many interlocking universes, and other pioneers have gone past his limits of speculation to their limits of credibility. Other universes suggest other dimensions based on laws beyond the comprehension of our scientists and beyond detection by our technology. Anything operating in this realm would appear to be magic to us and would of course be dismissed as a non-event or illusion by those who hold tenaciously to the limitations of existing science. But only a century ago electric light, radio, television and flight, let alone space flight, were in the realm of magic to all but the foolhardy.

If we read between the lines of religion and science fiction, and look a little less to science for the understanding of extra-terrestrial intelligence, we might be more successful. I suggest that NASA's array of radio telescopes can not see the wood for the trees. They are looking out there instead of right here! That intelligence is even willing to talk to us, if we are willing to listen. Perhaps if we were to ask these ETs about their existence and purpose, they might tell us, and also spell out why they do not make their presence globally known. The problem is that religion invites us to talk to God, but if we dare to claim that he has answered us back we are considered crazy.

Channelling is a means of communication whereby an individual enters a hypnotic or trance-like state and begins to speak or write in a form which differs from his or her normal communication both in style and content. The content of such communications is generally of the nature of cosmic revelation, spiritual teaching, or personal guidance. The terminology is frequently abstract, sometimes archaic, the accent may be foreign, the phraseology is often strange and the handwriting is invariably quite different from the person's normal script.

During a channelling session, which can last up to an hour or more, people present are usually able to ask questions and receive immediate answers. When the channel, or medium as they are sometimes called, returns to normal consciousness, they may have total, partial or no recall of what was said. It is generally accepted that the deeper the trance the less recall is available.

This phenomenon of channelling is uncomfortable for and unexplainable by mainstream scientists and psychologists, and is therefore ignored by them. If forced to confront it and provide an explanation, they will define it as a hoax or a hallucination, but be totally unable to substantiate either theory. At this point they become irrational and unscientific!

Channelling or mediumship is as old as the hills or has existed at least since the maidens of the Oracle at Delphi counselled the rulers and warriors of ancient Greece. In the 20th century the most common manifestation of it has been in numerous spiritualist churches around the country where congregants are 'reconnected with the spirit of loved ones who have passed on to the other side'. In the last decade, however, channelling has found new popularity in many circles. Middle-class Californians today, emboldened by Shirley Maclaine's disclosures, swap revelations from their channels, just as they compared insights from their psychoanalysts a year or two ago.

Clearly some channels have access to more wisdom than the rest. But where does it come from? Is it an unidentified subconscious well of knowledge in the channel's own mind? Is the channel a skilful actor, actress or con-artist? If any of the above, what is the motive, for very few of them make as much money as they would doing a conventional job? Is it a spirit masquerading as something more elevated? Is it an advanced alien civilization with the power to communicate telepathically at a great distance? Is it God, a messenger of God or of the devil? What or who is it that speaks to us?

When this question is asked of the source, the answer is generally too abstract, too grandiose or too unbelievable to lead anywhere useful, or it is deftly side-stepped. One is left with the quality of the message being the only criterion on which to assess the quality of the source. This is a new angle for us humans. We are accustomed to judging the quality of the saying by the reputation of the sayer. It forces us to take personal responsibility for our interpretation and understanding. This is in itself a well-known spiritual learning concept, which may explain the evasiveness of the source.

So what are the messages from these apparently high sources telling us? It will perhaps come as no surprise that the messages to humankind today are remarkably similar, but in modern idiom of course, to the messages of the ancient seers and biblical prophets. There is, however, an added sense of urgency for humanity to take responsibility for the human condition that we have created, to take better care of all living things, our fellow human beings, our animals and our environment, to take responsibility for the place that people on earth play in the universe, to recognize the impact that our negativity has on the whole universal lifecycle, to understand that we are not alone in the universe, that we come to earth to learn to balance spirit and matter, to know that the soul never dies and that the one God, a particle of whom is contained within every one of us, loves us regardless of our creed, colour, culture or condition.

It sounds to me like an urgent call for *cooperation* on a grand scale. That seems to be a good idea anyway, and I don't really care who's making the call!

15
Freedom

In the last chapter we went on a speculative fantasy ride from chaos to the cosmos – and more of it than you think might, in time, turn out to be virtually the reality. Meanwhile back at the ranch, how should we respond to the prospect of so much change and uncertainty? With fear, with excitement – or should we do what so many people do and put our heads in the sand? We certainly would not be alone down there, and it would be easier.

'I have my family, my mortgage and my ego to support, and that takes up most of my time. In fact, time appears to be accelerating so much that I can not even find the time to do the ordinary things I used to do, let alone play a round or two of golf each week – or try to change the world! Besides, what effect could I personally have, if I wanted to? I have no time, but I have no power either. I can not even purchase some new software or a travel ticket without getting it signed off by my boss. How can I affect the state of the world when I have so little control over my own daily destiny? What can anyone do?'

It is true that even prime ministers, presidents and princes seem more like victims than victors in the game of life on a planet in flux. However we can do a lot. We are not powerless and there is time.

Humanity and the country or company culture in which we operate is mainly *assertive*, but it is evolving towards *cooperation* at its own pace as we all evolve. Individually the impact each one of us can have may seem very small. We may feel that we can not change the circumstances, but we *can* change how we perceive and react to those circumstances – and we can change ourselves.

Although external material circumstances may be associated with each of the stages *inclusion, assertion* and *cooperation,* the terms as used in this book are socio-psychological in nature. They describe the state of mind of the individuals or groups to which I have applied them. The same is true of the more emotive terms, **need, greed** and **freedom**. **Need** suggests a lack of essentials, **greed** suggests an excess of non-essentials and **freedom** suggests an absence of constraints. Essentials, non-essentials and constraints exist in entirely physical form such as food, gold or chains, and can be approached at that level by the acquisition of the first two and the removal of the last. That may be a good place to start, like first aid, but true resolution only occurs when the causal feelings are resolved. This is evolutionary, and may take a little longer!

We have examined the characteristics of the *inclusion, assertion* and *cooperation* stages and how they manifest themselves in groups of all shapes and sizes, from family through sport and business to nations. We have seen how these stages are paralleled in Maslow's hierarchy of personal needs. The terms **need, greed** and **freedom** apply equally to individuals and to groups. It is also true that we have more direct experience of the first two stages than we do of the last, for the simple reason that that is about as high as humanity as a whole has climbed up the evolutionary tree so far. We all have had an experience or two of people behaving in *cooperation* with one another, but as yet that is far from the norm. In fact on the very odd occasion when a group achieves a very high-quality *cooperation*, participants frequently recognize that earlier experiences of apparent cooperation were probably not really cooperation at all.

Inclusion and *assertion* occur in groups naturally without a decision or choice by the group or the group leader. *Cooperation* is different because it is voluntary by its very nature. Conformity, which gives the appearance of *cooperation*, can be imposed or demanded, but it is very ineffective. *Cooperation* is a choice made by each participating individual and one that is rarely made before *inclusion* and *assertion* issues are largely resolved. An exception to this occurs in the case of the human response to a life-threatening crisis, anything from a small accident to a world war; but unfortunately when the crisis is over so is the *cooperation*.

The decision to *cooperate* with others for the greater good, in the absence of a crisis, requires a certain level of psychological maturity.

At minimum that means freedom from the tyranny of the social or self-imposed imperatives to which so many of us unconsciously subjugate our choices. The aspirations to social *cooperation* and personal **freedom** are inextricably intertwined. We will not be able to *cooperate* until we first find **freedom**.

Finding personal **freedom** empowers us to *cooperate*. It also empowers us to be an agent of change or an advocate of evolution. If this book is more than a map of social evolution, it is a call for action – and what more rewarding action can there be but freeing and empowering ourselves. It is appropriate, therefore, that this concluding chapter explores the journey to psychological **freedom**, free as far as is possible from psychological jargon.

One dimension of growth

The fact that this is about a journey towards **freedom** implies that we do not start out free. Perhaps we were **free** as little babies, but the conditioning soon sets in, acquired at first from our parents and then from our peers and the wider culture. 'Brave boys don't cry,' or 'It is not nice to do that,' 'You should do this' – well-meaning parental guidance, perhaps, but it starts up our control mechanisms.

Because we want to be accepted and *included* we strive to conform. We want to do it right. We want to be liked. We struggle with our self-doubt and our fears, but after a while we begin to *assert* ourselves. Crudely at first, more shrewdly later, we fight the battles of life. We win some, we lose some, and we collect a few more fears and compulsions, debts and possessions, and wants and obligations. We get sad or mad at ourselves, at others or at God for the way things are, and we are afraid to express and release those feelings, so we accumulate them too.

All this amounts to quite a burden which we now carry with us wherever we go, as it is all in our head. We don't even know how much of it is of our own making and how much was imposed. It makes no odds for we accepted it anyway, and now we are stuck with it. We are wedded to our past. Silently our need for *inclusion* and *assertion* has conditioned our beliefs, our attitudes and our behaviour. None of us escapes this conditioning which moulds us and forces us down the tube of life.

However, all is not lost. We can be self-aware, we can be attentive to our personal development, through listening to our own emotional needs, through being open to learn and to grow through life's experience. Through committed engagement at work or in sport, art or other special interest, through training and development courses at work or through individual psychological self-development, we are able to free ourselves from some of our burdensome imperatives. Our mental attic, however, has many dusty corners and even the most diligent and persistent psychological house cleaning will never free us from all the residual conditioning.

Some people sincerely believe that they never were conditioned or are not controlled by the conditioning they had. This demonstrates a lack of awareness, an inability to differentiate between driven and chosen behaviour, and perhaps a touch of arrogance, born of the fact that people hate to think that they are not in total conscious control of their behaviour. Some recognize the many consequences of their conditioning, but do not believe that they can do anything to change it. Others believe that they can, and therefore actively set about reducing its impact on their lives. In practice we rarely do more than learn to manage those parts of our conditioning that hinder or impede our path towards our identified outer and inner goals. However, even this much can feel like a great liberation.

Along with the mental house cleaning, there may be some physical work to do as well. As any psychotherapist will know, emotions and trauma are reflected in the body and some form of ongoing physical release may be helpful, like jogging, squash or a physical psychotherapy such as bioenergetics or Rolfing.

As we let go, step by step, so we become **free**. Life controls us less and we begin to control our lives more. We cease to be a victim to circumstances when we recognize that there are two components, not one. There is the circumstance, and there is our reaction to it. We may have little control over the circumstance, but we can have total control over our reaction to it.

Let me illustrate this by an example from the physical world of skiing. All skiers will recall the sensation of going rigid when unexpectedly confronted with a patch of hard ice in the snow. They fall on the ice. Reminded of just how painful ice can be, the next time they become even more rigid, and true to form they fall again. Few skiers recognize that it was not the ice that caused them to fall, but their reaction to it. In trying desperately to hang on to control, they lost it. When we are willing to let go of control, and in this case just keep skiing normally, we gain control. When we quit playing victim to the ice, we gain the ability to respond to it. **Freedom** is letting go, even on the slippery slopes of life.

So much for the beginnings of individual psychological **freedom**. Let us assume, for a moment, that we have climbed Maslow's hierarchy of needs to the point that we have resolved our belonging needs. What is life like? We are as comfortable on our own as we are in a crowd. We don't mind being alone in a pub, or taking a meal by ourselves in a restaurant. We are unaffected by standing alone at a party, or when the people on either side of us at the table are turned away from us and deep in conversation with their other neighbour. We are not hurt by not being invited to the party or not selected for the team. We enjoy being with others, but we do not need them.

Let us imagine we have now climbed another step and resolved our esteem needs too. We are no longer concerned about how other people may judge us by our appearance, clothing, age, colour or accent as we walk down the street, or shop or play. The rust spots or registration letter on our car do not matter. Our taste in physical surroundings, houses, cars, possessions, clothing, work and leisure activities becomes more authentic and often simpler. Money loses its significance as a symbol of power or status and is seen more as a form of energy. It all sounds easy, but it involves us in a protracted process of letting go.

We find that we can speak as easily to a hundred people from a lecture platform as we do in private to a close friend. We are not afraid to express our emotions, and we are not fazed by other people expressing theirs. Nothing embarrasses us; in fact we can, if called on to do so, make a fool of ourselves without feeling a fool. We are as at ease conversing with royalty, a person who is severely disabled or one who is dying, a movie star, a Cuban construction worker or an Australian aborigine, as we are with our sister. We act by absolute choice, not as the effect of any social or personal imperatives. This is **freedom**.

We are empowered by the freedom of choice we now have. We are totally responsible for every choice we make, because we make it consciously. We are not acting because society expects us to do so and so, or because our father would have wanted us to, had he been alive today. We take the helm of our own ship, rather than allow ourselves to be tossed around rudderless on the waves of our emotions, or by our expectations of those of others. We are acting out of clarity with intention, and consequently we are very effective at whatever we chose to do. This is an immensely powerful but quite unusual state for a normal mortal. It is the highest state on Maslow's hierarchy of needs, self-actualization, which means no more or less than becoming who we really or actually are.

I am fortunate to have had many friends and acquaintances who have achieved a lot in the eyes of, and by the terms of, our society. They have achieved in spite of the limiting effects of their conditioning. I have only one friend of whom I can safely say that his choices and his actions are entirely his own. He has produced extraordinary results in every one of the great variety of things he has done in business and for pleasure. Some of his achievements have not been recognized by others, some have been attributed to others, though in truth the achievement was his. He minds not one bit. No challenge daunts him, because he does not fear failure – so he does not fail. He is aware of what others have done before in similar circumstances, but he is neither impressed nor dismissive, he simply approaches every task as if it is a first. The unexpected never throws him. His objectives are crystal clear. Personal recognition and ego do not feature as motives, so his decisions are uncontaminated. He is always at peace with himself, and he is a devoted parent. He would not mind if I revealed his name here, neither will he mind that I don't.

In psychological terms this is known as being disidentified. It is a state of not being identified with one's possessions, qualifications, occupation, appearance or with one's achievements and failures. It also means not being identified with one's personality, one's mind, one's emotions or one's body. As we strip away these false identifications, we begin to uncover our true identity – to discover who we really are. When we know who we are, the labels that other people put on us, the judgements that other people make about us from our appearance, possessions or any other criteria, become unimportant to us. They cannot throw us off course, they do not affect us.

So what do we find beneath those discarded masks and façades? We find our true self. Christians call this the soul, some call it the higher self. I will call it the Self. It is our centre. It provides us with a sense of permanence, of continuity, of consistency and sameness which gives a true sense of security. This is an infinitely more complete security than the security of the personality, which we seek in our *inclusion* (belonging) and *assertion* (esteem) phases.

This permanence of the Self may in turn give us a new perspective on physical life and in particular on its temporary and transient nature. When we cease to be identified with our physical body, not only may our fear of death dissolve, but also the fear of fear in the face of pain or death. We begin to develop a knowing that life transcends physical death, that life is spiritual rather than physical in nature. This knowing is more profound than the belief of religionists and more convincing than the proof of scientists. It is a form of spiritual awakening that opens the door to whole new realms of spiritual experience.

Two dimensions of growth

I have referred earlier to psychosynthesis which is, in my opinion, the most progressive and inclusive strand in psychology today. By inclusive here I mean that it addresses both the psychological and the spiritual development of humanity, whereas the main body of psychology ignores the spiritual altogether, in the manner expected of scientific reductionism. Psychosynthesis also suggests that many of humanity's ills, both individually and collectively, can be attributed to a fundamental lack of meaning, which in our modern society has reached epidemic proportions.

Crisis of meaning
My experience of working with business people strongly confirms this. People at all levels of business today are asking themselves,

'What am I doing all this for?', 'What is the point of all this stress and activity?', 'Are there not better ways to live than the daily office fare?', 'What I am doing doesn't really seem to have any value or purpose, for me or for anyone else. Is this really how I want to spend my life?', 'What do I want to achieve? Is this it?', 'What is really meaningful in my life?', 'I push paper or a computer mouse around all day, for what, for whom?', 'I was optimistic and enthusiastic when I first started my work life, but now I can't wait to retire. What have I done with my life? What else could I have done with my life? What should I have done with my life?', *and most importantly*, 'What am I going to do with the rest of my life?'.

These are questions of personal meaning. They are psychological questions.

There are another set of questions which logically follow these, but which some people ask themselves and others steadfastly avoid. They are what can be described as spiritual questions such as: 'What is the meaning of life itself?', 'What is the ultimate purpose of life, not just my life, but all life?', 'What is the meaning of all the pain and suffering in the world?', 'Can or will humanity ever live in peace and harmony with itself?', 'What is the nature of the world we live in?', 'Why do we all live and love, work and worry, fear and fight, do and die, on this tiny speck of dust in a vast universe?', 'What is good and what is evil?', 'What is time, and what is space?', 'What is beyond both of them', 'Is there life after death?', 'Does God really exist?', 'What is consciousness?', 'Is humanity evolving to something better?'.

The search for meaning, both on a personal and on a spiritual level, is perhaps the most neglected need in daily life. This is Maslow's ultimate need for self-actualization, and for self-realization even beyond that. Humanity itself, postmodernists would agree, seems to have acquired an overdose of meaninglessness. It is such an obvious and pervasive crisis, yet we so easily ignore it or hide ourselves from it on the treadmill of our own personal rat race. Perhaps it is because we think that there are no answers or that we could never find them, so why bother? Perhaps facing these questions and their answers might require us to change, and that is too threatening and disruptive to our safe, familiar and excruciatingly boring and meaningless lives! Perhaps we hold back our questions because others seldom speak of them, and we are therefore too embarrassed to do so. Perhaps we all feel alone because we don't discuss these essential questions with one another. However, once they have arrived, they never fully go away again.

> Do we make plans and decisions in business without having determined the goal? Of course not – then why on earth do rational people do precisely that about the far more important business of life itself? How can we determine the direction of our lives unless we consider its purpose? Or are we just victims of life?

To attempt to clarify further the process of self-development and the journey towards personal freedom, I am going to use a diagram to represent the psychological and spiritual dimensions of growth and the search for meaning. Psychological development is on the horizontal plane, for which the scale can be marked in segments of time, steps along the journey towards psychological maturity, or as a series of personal achievements, from learning to ride a bicycle to landing a good job, to having a family or to finding satisfaction and happiness. People reaching the right-hand end of this line would be described as mature, having the capacity to function effectively in the world and to set and achieve personal goals. They would be reasonably disidentified from their conditioning. They would have a developed personal will, an integrated personality and a stable sense of identity.

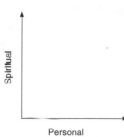

The vertical plane of the diagram is the spiritual dimension, better described as the transpersonal dimension for those to whom the word 'spiritual' has loaded connotations. In fact this realm is nothing to do with spirits and requires none of the belief of religion. The gradation marks up the vertical axis represent steps in the recognition of life's meaning and purpose, in achieving breadth and clarity of vision, in the development of transpersonal qualities such as compassion, wisdom, serenity, harmony and ultimately unity with all life, or rungs on the ladder towards enlightenment via freedom from the control of the material world and the capacity to transcend the personality.

These two dimensions are distinct but not separate. Growth along both is a natural and normal process of human development. Most people, however, are oriented towards one or the other, and see that as the most important, even to the extent of being unconscious of, denying or ignoring the other, or being highly critical of those who focus on the alternate. Both types are most likely to see the other as selfish. Let us consider an example of each.

A business person may be focused on personal achievement and success in the material world and may have become a well-integrated person, a good parent and a respected member of society, without ever having asked themselves a meaningful question about life. This is the tendency of western people, which has resulted in great material progress and innovation. They may be scornful of the more mystical type who leads a contemplative and ascetic life but who seems ill equipped to cope with the realities and essentials of the everyday world.

The latter type of person is more interested in 'subtle energies' than in the type of energy the business person produces and consumes. They live a monastic life of study and of gentle assistance to others. Their home, their finances and even their personality may be in a bit of a mess. However, they see the business person's pursuits as being pointless, ego driven, and often destructive to themselves and others. This is the eastern path; although given the economic growth of the East of late, these geographical distinctions are liable to be confusing.

The qualities of both of these ways have their value and, to become a fully self-realized being, the balanced integration of both is essential. Of course, this implies that there is an arrival point at the station called self-realization, but self-realizing is a journey without end. It can be said that the purpose of life is not to find the purpose of life, but to seek it.

The existential crisis

The singular pursuit of either way to the exclusion of the other is liable to lead to a crisis. For the achiever on the psychological journey the crisis is called the existential crisis. Rather than make any attempt to identify the components of this type of crisis, I will rely on the outstanding clarity of Leo Tolstoy about its occurrence in his life (as quoted in *Synthesis Journal*):

Increasing personality integration with no spiritual development

> Five years ago something very strange began to happen to me. At first I experienced moments of perplexity and arrest of life as though I did not know what to do or how to live, and I felt lost and became dejected. But this passed, and I went on living as before. Then these moments of perplexity began to recur more and more often. . . They were always expressed by the questions: What is it for? What does it lead to?
>
> At first it seemed to me that these were aimless and irrelevant questions. I thought that it was all well-known, and that if I should ever wish to deal with the solution it would not cost me much effort: just at present, I had no time for it, but when I wanted to I should be able to find the answer. The questions however began to repeat themselves frequently and to demand replies more and more insistently... I understood that it was something very important; and that if these questions constantly repeated themselves they would have to be answered. And I tried to answer them. The questions seemed such stupid, simple, childish ones; but as soon as I touched them and tried to solve them I at once became convinced, first, that they are not childish and stupid but the most important and profound of life's questions; and secondly that, try as I would, I could not solve them.
>
> All around me I had what is considered complete good fortune. I was not yet fifty; I had a good wife who loved me and whom I loved, good children, and a large estate which without much effort on my part improved and increased. I was respected by my relations and acquaintances more than at any previous time. I was praised by others and without much self-deception could consider that my name was famous. And far from being insane or mentally diseased, I enjoyed on the contrary a strength of mind and body such as I have seldom met with among men of my kind;

physically I could keep up with the peasants at mowing, and mentally I could work for eight and ten hours at a stretch without experiencing any ill results from such exertion.

I felt that what I had been standing on had collapsed, and that I had nothing left under my feet. What I had lived on no longer existed, and there was nothing left.

My life came to a standstill. I could breathe, eat, drink, and sleep, and I could not help doing these things; but there was no life, for there were no wishes the fulfillment of which I could consider reasonable. If I desired anything, I knew in advance that whether I satisfied my desire or not, nothing would come of it. Had a fairy come and offered to fulfill my desires I should not have known what to ask. If in moments of intoxication I felt something which, though not a wish, was a habit left by former wishes, in sober moments I knew this to be a delusion and that there was really nothing to wish for.

The resolution of the existential crisis occurs when a person is able to expand the meaning of his or her existence beyond the boundaries of his or her own personality. This inevitably leads to an exploration of the transpersonal or spiritual dimension of life. It is as if the magnetic power of the Self increases and draws the person towards it. As he or she now moves up the vertical plane, his or her lack of meaning is replaced by a sense that there is something missing which needs to be found, and a search begins.

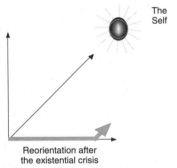

The Self

Reorientation after the existential crisis

A recall and reinterpretation may occur of early random spiritual moments or peak experiences, even from childhood, and a curiosity about the mystical or the unexplained in life or in our world may develop. At the same time, the process mentioned earlier of disidentifying from the personality and its limitations continues, along with a letting go of one's psychological history. This is not a question of killing off the personality but rather integrating it into what is now recognized as a much greater whole, the unity of life. A sense of

meaning and purpose is restored but with a
hugely expanded vision and renewed energy to act in the world for the greater good.

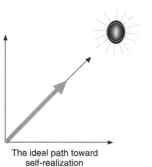

The ideal path toward
self-realization

At this point one is back on track and
progress upward and forward can be maintained. Of course, this whole process many
occur as a bumpy ride through a series of
mini-crises or as a single leap such as
Tolstoy experienced. The ideal in life
would seem to be consistent progress
upward and forward at 45 degrees on our graph from childhood
onwards, but this is rare indeed.

More often in life, we progress not through following the best
track, but through bouncing off the guard rails. At the opposite side
of the track from the existential crisis lies the potential for another
crisis.

The crisis of duality

This kind of crisis most commonly
occurs to those who from quite early in
life attempt to follow a spiritual path,
or to those who feel chronically discon-
tented with life and/or driven by an
undifferentiated imperative. This may
be experienced not only by monks and
ascetics, but also by ordinary people
who are more mystical or artistic in

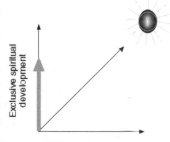

nature, or who merely lack grounding. The form this crisis usually
takes is that initial fast progress up the vertical axis becomes increasingly frustrated or appears to be barred altogether.

The duality is the experience of the gulf which exists between the
clarifying vision of the potential of humankind for joy, for compassion, for fulfilment and for *cooperative* harmony, and the reality of
pain, of deprivation, of **need** and of **greed**. Depression and frustration
grow as individuals experience their own impotence to effect any

change in the world, and the realization that contemplation and understanding alone do not bring about change. This may be the catalyst which forces a reorientation towards the development of a more effective personality, better equipped to cope with the world as it is. A switch from the abstract to mundane and physical activities may be needed to assist people to become more solidly grounded or centred. As they become more effective and gain psychological strength and confidence, they may once more reintegrate their spirituality into everyday life, leading to better balanced progress upwards and forward in future. Again, this process may occur in any number of ways from a series of highs and lows, to a single monumental crisis.

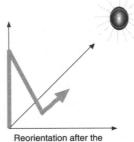

Reorientation after the
crisis of duality

People who actively engage in self-development and are aware of the stages involved may at times seek the support of a skilled counsellor to help them prevent these crises from occurring, to minimize their negative impact if they do and, as far as possible, to encourage progressive evolution. Life, however, is not going to be perfect, painless and permanently fulfilling from the first flash of the possibility of self-realization. There will be lapses, needs, moments of doubt and insecurity, but the knowing remains that they too will pass, and that they are not who you are. Your fundamental alrightness is not affected by them. It must be appreciated that one is likely to experience some discomfort on any lengthy journey, and the choice to embark on the journey at all must be taken with that awareness. Of course, this is to some extent a natural, involuntary, unconscious, evolutionary process which may creep up unawares.

Rather than being entirely fuelled by the evolutionary thrust from below, Dr Roberto Assagioli (the founder of psychosynthesis) postulated that the Self acts as a magnet to draw us up the evolutionary mountain. More precisely, he suggested that the Self poured down superconscious energies to infuse the personality at suitable moments to strengthen it and provide direction for its onward journey. Whether this actually occurs or is merely a metaphor matters not, for it graphically serves to assist our understanding of the feelings associated with the experience.

With the growing concern that a self-
realizing person experiences for the greater
whole, for humanity and for our planet, a
refocusing of priorities will invariably
occur. Such people will want their life to be
an expression of their values and they may
no longer wish to fritter their lives away on
mindless, selfish or materialistic activities.
Just creating more meaningful leisure time
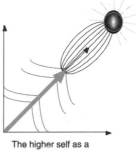
The higher self as a
magnet

alone is unlikely to be enough. Whereas in the past work and play
may have been seen as quite separate, now, just as play shifts towards
service and contribution to others, there is a desire for work time to
reflect the same values. This may result in further questions about the
futility, the ethics and the beneficiaries of a person's necessary work
life, which not infrequently leads to a change of job to another one
of greater social benefit, even at lower pay, but one which is infinitely more fulfilling.

Just as breathing is a natural activity of our body, service is a natural activity of our Higher Self – and at a certain point of development, it becomes
natural to the personality as well. Its precursor in the personality is the
urge to make things better. This is perhaps our most human tendency, that
which most clearly distinguishes man from animal. And as we make contact with the superconscious and begin to understand the larger whole as
it is and as it is evolving, we are spontaneously drawn to use our energies
to assist that evolution, to help the gradual work of perfecting man and his
world. We recognize that service in line with our transpersonal vision is the
most effective way to make things better, the most meaningful thing to do.

John Firman and James Vargiu wrote this in an article entitled
'Dimensions of growth' (*Synthesis Journal*, 1976). They go on to suggest that personal development and a life of service merge to become
one and the same thing, and far from being one of self-denial, it is
one that brings great joy:

The integrative path of Self-Realization has in it an inherent *joyousness*. It is the joy of becoming who we really are by living our higher values – the joy of *Self*-expression. It arises from the increasingly immediate sense of our true identity, as we learn to manifest it in daily life. We realize that as the Self, we are one with the larger whole, that our essential nature is what we would have to describe by such words as 'transcendent', 'immortal', 'divine'. Yet we deal with such joyous realizations realistically, because we so understand our need to progressively cooperate with and find our place in the larger context, as it is continuously revealed to us.

Conclusion

In this last chapter we have made a little excursion into the outer limits of an evolved individual consciousness, which seems far removed from the sorry state of collective consciousness we experience around us. Western civilization is, however, drawing ever closer to the transformative shift from *assertion* to *cooperation*.

As individuals and humanity at large evolve psychospiritually step by step, business leaders, educationalists and those in government will sooner or later have to take these trends into consideration. Right now, however, the economic power of the major corporations is very apparent and pervasive as the *assertion* stage peaks. Few political or business leaders have much understanding of, capacity for or allocate any budget to developing a real long-term vision, taking into account the evolving nature of human consciousness. The evidence is at the moment that most are too busy trying to plug the hole in their boat to notice that it is drifting ever faster towards the weir.

Awareness
As change continues to accelerate exponentially, the need to anticipate the form and nature of social change becomes ever greater. The more perceptive have already seen the vanguard of the *cooperation* stage waiting in the wings. It is the power of ordinary evolving people which is emerging everywhere to challenge and to question the old *assertive*

order, to demand more ethical and compassionate standards in political and business life, to reject the commercial hype that lowered the tone of the 1996 Atlanta Olympics, and to care for our world and all its flora and fauna. The Berlin Wall came down and so are office partitions – the time is coming to remove the inner walls that segregate us from our neighbours and from our selves.

The tide of social evolution is inevitable and inexorable, and it comes in waves. The ebb between the waves could deceive the glance of a casual observer. Truly to trust the direction of the tide we have to pay a little more attention. To reverse the direction of the tide is impossible, but there will always be those who try. If they don't pay attention, they may be swept aside by a sudden unexpected tidal wave of transformation. Any nation or multinational corporation, any politician or executive, any country or company, any religion or cult, any teacher or parent, any scientist or psychologist, any individual or group whose life or work runs counter to the principles of freedom of self and of others, or contrary to the principles of *cooperation*, is swimming against the tide.

For this we need <u>awareness</u>. <u>Awareness</u> needs to be open, brutally honest, continuously alert and of a high definition. <u>Awareness</u> means paying attention. Without <u>awareness</u> it is impossible to find the map or the path or even to know that either exist. Without self-<u>awareness</u> it is impossible to recognize the **needs** and **greed** that obscure the way.

Responsibility

Individual development, however, can not and should never be removed from the absolute choice of the individual; however much we might all collectively benefit from the effects of some kind of National Evolution Service, the idea is positively Orwellian. We can not and should not be dependent on or deterred by any external authority, great or small, in our personal evolution. Our company, our country, our church or any individual, even our guru, is powerless to do it for us, or to stop us doing it for ourselves. They can restrict our physical freedom, and they may try to force us down a particular path of their choosing, but they actually have no control whatsoever over our own psychospiritual freedom. We can choose to join the culture change, to use the business jargon, or we can resist it.

We can work to free ourselves and others, or we can remain in the
prison of our own mind and of our own making. We can choose to
cooperate with others for all, or go it alone for ourselves.

<u>Responsibility</u> is important here. <u>Responsibility</u> needs to be chosen
not imposed, brutally honest also, and one hundred percent. Without
<u>responsibility</u> it is impossible to push through when the journey
becomes lonely or painful. Without <u>responsibility</u> there is no commitment, no motivation and no energy.

These are broadbrush concepts and this book is not intended to be
more than a large-scale map. However grand, illuminated or detailed,
maps are most often used for an individual journey and I hope this
simple one will help you for a step or two on your travels. I have no
precise prescription for you, but even if I did I wouldn't give it here,
because no one can know another person's path. Each individual has
in his or her heart a detailed map of his or her own personal path. All
he or she has to do is to find it. The map is obscured and the search
is hindered by **need** and **greed**. As these fall away the map and the

 path become clear. At best no more than a few steps
ahead are revealed at any time. That is enough to
enable us to move forward, and to learn to trust that
the next revelation will come when the time is right.

The path passes through a few briar patches, but
the journey towards personal **freedom**, when
embarked on consciously, expands our vision,
empowers our action and enriches our experience of
life so much that the scratches are a small price to pay.
There is no rose without thorns.

Bibliography

Peter Block (1993) *Stewardship*, Berrett-Koehler, San Francisco, USA

Sue Cartwright and Cary Cooper (1988) *No Hassle*, Penguin, Harmondsworth, UK

Noam Chomsky (1985) *Turning the Tide*, Pluto, London, UK

Deepak Chopra (1996) *The Seven Spiritual Laws*, Bantam, London, UK

Kenneth Clark (1969) *Civilisation*, BBC/John Murray, London, UK

Leslie Cockburn (1988) *Out of Control*, Bloomsbury, London, UK

Cary Cooper (1988) *Living with Stress*, Penguin, Harmondsworth, UK

Stephen Covey (1995) *First Things First*, Fireside, New York, USA

William Davis (1996) *The Lucky Generation*, Headline, London, UK

Rupert Eales-White (1995) *Building Your Team*, Kogan Page, London, UK

Jerry Fletcher (1993) *Patterns of High Performance*, Berrett-Koehler, San Francisco, USA

Viktor E Frankl (1973) *The Doctor and the Soul*, Vintage Books, New York, USA

Tim Gallwey (1975) *The Inner Game of Tennis*, Cape, London, UK

Jim Garrison (1983) *The Russian Threat*, Gateway, Bath, UK

Daniel Goleman (1995) *Emotional Intelligence*, Bantam, London, UK

Al Gore (1993) *Earth in the Balance*, Plume, New York, USA

Charles Handy (1995) *Beyond Certainty*, Hutchinson, London, UK

Robert Hargrove (1995) *Masterful Coaching*, Pfeiffer, San Diego, USA

Roger Harrison (1995) *The Collected Papers of Roger Harrison*, McGraw Hill, Maidenhead, UK

Paul Hawken (1993) *The Ecology of Commerce*, HarperBusiness, New York, USA

David Hemery (1991) *Sporting Excellence*, Collins Willow, London, UK

Francis Kinsman (1983) *The New Agenda*, Spencer Stuart, London, UK

Francis Kinsman (1990) *Millennium*, Penguin, Harmondsworth, UK

Alfie Kohn (1993) *Punished by Rewards*, Houghton Mifflin, Boston, USA

Robert Kriegel (1996) *Sacred Cows*, Warner, New York, USA

Max Lansberg (1996) *The Tao of Coaching*, HarperCollins, London, UK

James Lovelock (1991) *Gaia*, Gaia, London, UK

John E Mack (1994) *Abduction*, Scribner's, New York, USA

Abraham Maslow (1971) *The Farther Reaches of Human Nature*, Penguin, Harmondsworth, UK

John Naisbitt (1995) *Global Paradox*, Nicholas Brealey, London, UK

Eric Parsloe (1992) *Coaching, Mentoring and Assessing*, Kogan Page, London, UK

Scott Peck (1978) *The Road Less Travelled*, Touchstone, New York, USA

Abraham Ralph (1994) *Chaos, Gaia, Eros*, HarperCollins, London, UK

Salman Rushdie (1987) *The Jaguar Smile*, Picador, London, UK

Peter Russell (1982) *The Awakening Earth*, Routledge, London, UK

Phyllis Schlemmer (1993) *The Only Planet of Choice*, Gateway, Bath, UK

Ricardo Semler (1993) *Maverick*, Century, London, UK

Rupert Sheldrake (1987) *A New Science of Life*, HarperCollins, London, UK

Alex Walker (1994) *The Kingdom Within*, Findhorn Press, Inverness, UK

Margaret Wheatley (1994) *Leadership and the New Science*, Berrett-Koehler, San Francisco, USA

Margaret Wheatley and Myron Kellner-Rogers (1996) *A Simpler Way*, Berrett-Koehler, San Francisco, USA

Larry C White (1988) *Merchants of Death*, Beech Tree Books/Morrow, New York, USA

Diana Whitmore (1991) *Psychosynthesis Counselling*, Sage, London, UK

John Whitmore (1996) *Coaching for Performance*, 2nd edn, Nicholas Brealey, London, UK

Ken Wilber (1995) *Sex, Ecology, Spirituality*, Shambhala, Boston, USA

Anything and everything by Loren Eiseley, Clive James, John Pilger and Lyall Watson

Useful Addresses

Action on Smoking and Health
Devon House
12–15 Dartmouth Street
London SW1I 9BL
UK
Tel: (0)171 314 1360

Campaign against the Arms Trade
11 Goodwin Street
Finsbury Park
London N4 3HQ
UK
Tel: (0)171 281 0297
Fax: (0)171 281 4369

Consumers' Association
2 Marylebone Road
London NW1 4DF
UK
Tel: (0)171 830 6000
Fax: (0)171 830 6220

Esalen Institute
Big Sur
CA 93920
USA
Tel: (408) 667 2335

Ethical Consumer
ECRA Publishing Ltd
16 Nicholas Street
Manchester M1 4EJ
UK
Tel: (0)161 237 1630
Fax: (0)161 228 2347

Findhorn Foundation
The Park, Findhorn
Forres, Nr Inverness
IV36 0TZ
UK
Tel: (0)1309 690311

Greenpeace
Canonbury Villas
London N1 2PN
UK
Tel: (0)171 354 5100
Fax: (0)171 696 0012

Performance Consultants
Suite 1
Gregories Court, Gregories Road
Beaconsfield
Bucks HP9 1HQ
UK
Tel: (0)1494 670505
Fax: (0)1494 672263

Psychosynthesis & Education
Trust
92/94 Tooley St
London Bridge
London SE1 2TH
UK
Tel: (0)171 403 2100
Fax: (0)171 403 5562

Schumacher College
The Old Postern
Dartington
Totnes
Devon TQ9 6EA
UK
Tel: (0)1803 865934
Fax: (0)1803 866899

To order the book *Millennium 2000* send £5.75 (includes postage and packing) to:
Francis Kinsman
4 Sion Hill Place
Bath
Somerset BA1 5SJ
UK

Index